My Southern Cooking

Classic Southern Recipes
from Truly Southern Families

cookbook
resources LLC

Miss Sadie's Southern Cooking

1st Printing July 2005

Hard Cover: ISBN # 1-931294-67-4
Library of Congress Number: 2005903537

Edited, Designed and Published in the
United States of America and
Manufactured in China by
Cookbook Resources, LLC
541 Doubletree Drive
Highland Village, Texas 75077

Toll free 866-229-2665
www.cookbookresources.com

cookbook resources® LLC

Introduction
A Taste Of The South

Food and hospitality go hand in hand in the South. From its agricultural beginnings, the South has gained its reputation for good food and good times very honestly. It was common to entertain family and friends surrounded with big tables filled with the best fruits, vegetables and meats the land had to offer.

Historians love to trace the history of foods and dishes because they have such colorful beginnings. During its plantation heyday, slaves did most of the cooking, and they used seasonings and techniques that came with them from Africa. Today, the same seasonings and techniques are still used and they continue to preserve the rich cultural mix of the South.

It is easy to describe the South from its food because the agricultural and coastal wealth of the region provides such variety. We incorporate this variety in our cookbook so that the region's personality shines through.

Salted and smoked hams, fried chicken, fried green tomatoes, a mess o' greens, sweet potatoes, pecan pie, barbeque, steamed oysters, soft-shell crabs, sweet tea and grits are easily recognized as belonging to the South.

We collected authentic southern recipes so you, too, can taste and enjoy some goodness that is unmistakably southern.

Meet Miss Sadie.

Miss Sadie sits on the front porch of her antebellum home and waves at the passers-by. Although she doesn't know everyone in town like she once did, everyone knows her. She was the belle of the ball in her day. Her fried chicken, biscuits and gravy and fried peach pies were the envy of the town.

Miss Sadie's seen almost as much history as her 100-year-old home. A Southerner through and through, she knows the South. Thanks to some of her well-preserved history, facts and wisdom shared in the pages of the cookbook, we catch a glimpse of the old South.

Contents

Contents

Sunny Appetizers
and
Happy Beverages

Candied Pecans

1 (16 ounce) box light brown sugar
2 teaspoons cinnamon
½ cup water
1 teaspoon vanilla
4 cups pecan halves

In medium saucepan, combine sugar and cinnamon and add water. Cook until mixture reaches soft-ball stage when dropped into cold water.

Cook 15 minutes and add vanilla and pecan halves. Stir until pecans coat well and syrup is thick. Pour immediately onto wax paper and separate halves immediately. Store in sealed container.

Virginia Hot Dip

1 cup chopped pecans
2 teaspoons butter
2 (8 ounce) package cream cheese, softened
4 tablespoons milk
5 ounces dried beef, minced
1½ teaspoons garlic salt
1 cup sour cream
2 tablespoons finely minced onion
1 teaspoon hot sauce

Preheat oven to 350°. Saute pecans in butter and set aside. In mixing bowl, combine remaining ingredients and mix thoroughly. Place in sprayed, shallow baking dish and bake uncovered for 20 minutes. Remove from oven and sprinkle sautéed pecans over top. Serve hot with crackers or small breadsticks.

Cheesy Pecan Spread

2 tablespoons milk
1 (8 ounce) package cream cheese
1 (2½ ounce) jar dried beef, shredded
2 tablespoons dried onion flakes
¼ teaspoon pepper
¼ cup red bell pepper, finely chopped
¼ teaspoon garlic powder
½ cup sour cream
2 tablespoons (¼ stick) butter
½ cup chopped pecans

Preheat oven to 325°. In mixing bowl, combine cream cheese and milk and blend until smooth. Add beef, onion flakes, seasonings and bell pepper. Fold in sour cream. Spread mixture in shallow baking dish.

In saucepan with butter, heat pecans over low heat. Remove from heat, sprinkle over cheese mixture and bake for 30 minutes. Spread on crackers or melba toast rounds.

The fall harvest is the best time to buy pecans in the South.

Fried Cheese-Grits Party Bites

1 cup quick-cooking grits
1½ cups extra sharp, shredded American cheese
1 egg, slightly beaten
Dash cayenne red pepper, optional
Shortening
Flour

Cook grits according to package directions. Remove from burner when done and stir in cheese and egg. Continue to stir until cheese melts. Add cayenne pepper to taste.

Pour grits into large, shallow dish. Grits should not be more than ½-inch thick in dish. When completely cool, chill for several hours or overnight.

When ready to serve, cut grits into bite-size slices. Place in paper bag containing enough flour to coat grits when shaken. Deep-fry in hot shortening until golden brown. Drain well and serve immediately.

Grits became the Official Prepared Food of Georgia in 2002. They are made from bits of ground corn or hominy and are used as a breakfast dish or side dish.

Peanut Butter Crisps

1 loaf thin-sliced bread
1½ cups peanut butter
1½ cups vegetable oil
Parsley flakes
Crazy salt
Seasoned salt

Preheat oven to 250°. Remove crusts from each slice of bread and cut slices into 4 strips. Place all strips on 1 baking sheet and all crusts and heels on separate baking sheet. Place both baking sheets in oven and bake for 1 hour.

When toasted, place crusts in blender and make crumbs. Mix oil and peanut butter until smooth. Mix crumbs with parsley flakes, crazy salt, seasoned salt or any other flavored salt or herb of choice. (Use a light touch with salt so crumbs will not get too salty.)

Dip strips into oil mixture and roll in crumbs. Dry on wax paper and store in tightly covered container or freeze.

Tip: This freezes well so you can make it in advance and enjoy your free time.

By law, peanut butter must have at least 90% peanuts.
If the percentage is less, the product is called peanut spread.

Angels on Horseback

12 slices bacon
1 pint oysters, well-drained
Toothpicks
Salt, pepper, paprika to taste
Parsley

Preheat oven to 350°. Cut bacon into same number of pieces oysters. Wrap bacon around oysters. Secure with toothpicks.

Sprinkle each oyster with salt, pepper and paprika. Place rack on shallow baking pan and brown slowly for about 15 to 20 minutes. Serve on bed of parsley.

Oyster Tidbits

1 (5 ounce) can smoked oysters, drained, chopped
½ cup herb-seasoned stuffing mix
¼ cup water
8 slices bacon, halved, partially cooked

Preheat oven to 350°. In bowl, combine oysters, stuffing mix and water. Form into balls, using 1 heaping tablespoon mixture for each.

Wrap half slice bacon around each ball and secure with toothpick. Place on rack in shallow baking pan and cook for 25 to 30 minutes. Drain on paper towels.

Crab Bites

This recipe is a scrumptious dish. Serve as hors d'oeuvre or luncheon sandwich.

1 (7 ounce) can claw crab
1 cup (2 sticks) butter, softened
1 (5 ounce) jar sharp Old English cheese
½ teaspoon garlic salt or seasoned salt
2 tablespoons mayonnaise
2 dashes Worcestershire sauce
6 English split muffins

Preheat oven to 400°. In bowl, blend crab, butter, cheese, seasoning, mayonnaise and Worcestershire sauce into paste. Spread on muffins. Bake for 10 to 15 minutes or until brown.

Tip: Each muffin may be cut into 8 bite-size pieces or left whole and frozen.

Quickie Clam Dip

1 (8 ounce) package cream cheese, softened
½ cup sour cream
4 green onions with tops, chopped
2 tablespoons ketchup
1 teaspoon Worcestershire sauce
1 teaspoon seasoned salt
1 (6 ounce) can minced clams

In bowl, blend all ingredients except clams. Drain clams, but do not wash. Mix clams into cream cheese mixture.

Southerner's Favorite Crab Dip

2 (8 ounce) packages cream cheese, softened
2 tablespoons milk
1 tablespoon prepared horseradish
2 (6 ounce) cans crabmeat, drained
1 bunch fresh green onions, minced, divided
1 teaspoon garlic salt
⅓ cup slivered almonds, toasted

Preheat oven to 350°. In mixing bowl, beat cream cheese, milk and horseradish. Fold in crabmeat, ½ green onions and garlic salt.

Pour mixture into shallow 9 x 9-inch baking dish and top with remaining onions and almonds. Bake for 20 minutes and serve with wheat crackers.

Barney's Boiled Peanuts

Usually only true Southerners go for these authentic
and traditional boiled peanuts. Yes, boiled.

Raw peanuts
Water
Salt

Pour enough water into large saucepan to cover peanuts. Add a little salt and boil for about 30 minutes. Taste to see if peanuts are done. They should have consistency of a cooked, dried bean. Add a little more salt, if needed.

If peanuts are not done, keep boiling and taste every 5 to 10 minutes. Drain peanuts and serve hot or chilled. Store in refrigerator.

Chicken Liver Bits

½ cup cornmeal
⅓ cup flour
1 teaspoon garlic salt
⅛ teaspoon pepper
8 chicken livers, cut into ½-inch pieces
1 egg
2 tablespoons milk
Oil

In shallow bowl, combine cornmeal, flour, salt, garlic salt and pepper. Sprinkle livers with additional salt and pepper. In separate bowl, mix egg with milk.

Dip each liver piece first into cornmeal mixture, then into egg mixture and again into cornmeal mixture. Be sure to coat each piece well. Fry liver pieces in deep, hot oil for 2 minutes or until golden brown. Insert toothpicks and serve hot.

Cranberry Punch

*This makes a delicious, light pink punch and that
is wonderful for weddings or parties.*

2 (28 ounce) bottles ginger ale
1 (46 ounce) can pineapple juice
1 (1 quart) jar cranberry juice
1 (1 quart) carton pineapple sherbet

Chill all ingredients. Mix in punch bowl.

Peach Delight

6 ounces pink lemonade concentrate, thawed
6 ounces vodka
6 ounces water
3 to 4 peaches, pitted, peeled
Crushed ice

Place lemonade, vodka, water and peaches in blender. Mix well.
Add crushed ice and blend until smooth.

Mary Opal's Reception Punch

4 cups sugar
6 cups water
5 ripe bananas, mashed
Juice of 2 lemons
1 (46 ounce) can pineapple juice
1 (6 ounce) can frozen concentrated orange juice
2 quarts ginger ale

Boil sugar and water for 3 minutes in saucepan over low heat. Cool. In mixing bowl, blend bananas with lemon juice and add pineapple and orange juice.

Combine all ingredients except ginger ale and freeze in large container. To serve, thaw for 1 hour, 30 minutes then add ginger ale. Punch will be slushy.

Wassail

Double the recipe for a holiday party.

4 (1 quart) jars apple cider
4 (6 ounce) cans frozen lemonade
1 tablespoon ground cloves
4 sticks cinnamon
½ teaspoon ground allspice

Heat ingredients and boil for 10 to 15 minutes. Serve hot.

Fresh Lemonade

14 to 16 lemons
3 quarts water
1½ to 2 cups sugar

Squeeze lemons into large pitcher with cold water. Add sugar and stir well. Serve over cracked ice. Store in refrigerator.

Southerner's Sweet Tea

If you order tea in the South, you'll probably get sweet tea. So if you want hot tea or unsweetened tea, be sure to specify. The real way to make tea is to use actual tea leaves or tea bags. Instant tea, dry concentrate and even canned teas don't qualify for true Southern sweet tea.

8 cups water, divided
4 teaspoons bulk tea
1¼ to 1½ cups sugar

Boil 4 cups water in glass pot, add tea and remove from heat. Steep covered for 10 to 15 minutes.

Pour remaining 4 cups cold water into pitcher and add sugar. Pour tea through strainer into pitcher and serve over lots of ice. Garnish with sprig of mint.

Summertime Iced Tea

6 cups water
1 cup sugar
6 to 8 small tea bags
6 sprigs fresh mint
½ cup orange juice
¼ cup lemon juice

In saucepan, bring water to boil. Add sugar, tea bags and mint and steep for 5 minutes. Remove tea bags and mint and let cool. Add orange and lemon and stir well.

Chill well before serving.

Instant Spiced Tea Mix

1 (9 ounce) jar Tang
½ cup instant lemonade mix
1½ cups sugar
1 cup instant tea mix
2 teaspoons cinnamon
1 teaspoon cloves

In large bowl, combine all ingredients and mix well. Store in sealed container and SHAKE WELL before using.

Use about 2 teaspoons per cup of boiling water.

Tip: Mixture can be stored for about 8 months.

Jim Bo's Kentucky Tea

3 tea bags
5 cups water, divided
1¼ cups sugar
1 (6 ounce) can frozen orange juice concentrate
½ (6 ounce) can frozen lemon juice concentrate
¾ cup bourbon

Add tea bags to 1½ cups water, bring to boil and steep for
5 minutes. Remove tea bags, add remaining ingredients and stir
until sugar dissolves.

Place in freezer for about 30 minutes to 1 hour. Scoop slushy
drink into tall glasses and garnish with lemon slices.

---

*Bourbon (or whiskey) originated in Bourbon County,
Kentucky. The U.S. government recognized it as uniquely
American in 1964 and is now protected by law.*

*Good bourbon can be used to replace brandy
in most recipes. Bourbon is used in sauces for
desserts, main dishes and barbeque sauces.*

*In the late 1780's, Reverend Elijah Craig, a Baptist minister,
developed corn liquor or bourbon whiskey in Kentucky.*

Kentucky Mint Julep
Official drink of the Kentucky Derby!

2 cups water
2 cups sugar
¼ cup fresh mint leaves
2 ounces Kentucky bourbon

In saucepan, cook water and sugar over medium to high heat for several minutes and stir constantly. Remove from heat and drop mint leaves in pan. Cover and steam for 30 minutes. Set aside and cool.

Place cracked ice in glass, pour Kentucky bourbon and 3½ ounces sugar-syrup mixture. Stir well and garnish with mint leaves and serve with straw.

Tip: Southerner's don't like to crush the mint in a julep.

The first Kentucky Derby was held in 1875 and has grown in popularity each year since then. More thoroughbred foals come from Kentucky than any other state in the U.S.

Summertime Brandy Julep

1 teaspoon sugar
1 tablespoon water
12 mint sprigs, divided
½ cup brandy
2 teaspoons light rum
Fresh pineapple for garnish

In separate glass, dissolve sugar and water. Add 6 sprigs of mint and stir vigorously to mix. Add brandy and stir.

Pack separate old–fashioned glass with crushed ice. Pour in brandy mixture and stir. Add rum and stir. Place glass in freezer for about 30 minutes to frost glass.

Decorate with pineapple slice, lime slice or other fresh fruit and remaining mint leaves.

Southern Rum Punch

½ cup pineapple juice
½ cup orange juice
½ cup lime juice
8 dashes Angostura bitters
1 cup (6 ounces) rum
½ cup corn syrup

Combine ingredients and shake well. Serve in tall glasses over crushed ice.

Warm-Your-Soul
Soups
and
Stylish Salads

Ham and Fresh Okra Soup

1 ham hock bone
1½ quarts water
1 cup frozen butter beans or lima beans
1½ pounds chicken or ham, cooked, cubed
1 (15 ounce) can chopped, stewed tomatoes
3 cups small, whole okra
2 large onions, diced
Salt
Pepper

Boil ham hock in water for about 1 hour, 30 minutes. Add
remaining ingredients and boil for 1 more hour. Serve over rice.

Quick and Easy Peanut Soup

¼ cup (½ stick) butter
1 onion, finely chopped
2 ribs celery, chopped
2 (10 ounce) cans cream of chicken soup
2 soup cans milk
1¼ cups crunchy-style peanut butter

Melt butter in saucepan and sauté onion and celery over low heat.
Blend in soup and milk and stir. Add peanut butter and continue
to heat until mixture blends well.

Slow-Cook
Navy Bean and Ham Soup
Better than Grandma's!

1½ cups dry navy beans
5 cups water
1 carrot, finely chopped
¼ cup celery, finely chopped
1 small onion, finely chopped
1 (¾ pound) ham hock
½ teaspoon salt
Dash pepper

Soak beans for 8 to 12 hours and drain. Place all ingredients in 2-quart slow cooker. Cook for 8 to 10 hours on LOW setting.

Remove ham hock and discard skin, fat and bone. Cut meat in small pieces and place in soup. Beans can be mashed if desired.

Miss Sadie: "Southerner's love a good pot o' beans. 'Course you have to season 'em right nice with some good ole country-cured ham or some smoked pork trimmins'. I guess our favorites start with black-eyed peas, maybe butter beans, but then limas aren't too bad. If you asked a Southerner about a pot o' beans, you'll get an ear full, that's for sure."

Edna Earle's Cold Peach Soup

This is delicious for summer luncheons with
vegetables or chicken salad sandwiches.

2 pounds peaches
1 tablespoon lemon juice
3 tablespoons quick-cooking tapioca
3 tablespoons sugar
Dash of salt
2½ cups water, divided
1 (6 ounce) can frozen orange juice concentrate

Puree peaches with lemon juice and set aside. Combine tapioca, sugar, salt and 1 cup water. Heat to full boil in saucepan and stir constantly.

Transfer to medium-sized bowl. Stir in orange juice until it melts. Add remaining 1½ cups water and stir until smooth. Mix in pureed peaches, cover and chill. Serve cold.

Tip: Make this soup before you need it so it has time to chill.

Georgia is ranked 3rd in production of peaches with most
being harvested between May and August.

Carolina She-Crab Soup

4 cups milk
¼ teaspoon mace
1 teaspoon lemon zest
1 pound crabmeat, flaked
2 (1 pint) cartons whipping cream
¼ cup (½ stick) butter
½ cup cracker crumbs, divided
Salt and white pepper
2 tablespoons sherry

Pour milk, mace and lemon zest in double boiler and simmer for 5 minutes. Add crabmeat, cream and butter and cook over low heat for 15 minutes.

Stir in cracker crumbs a little at a time to get consistency desired and season soup with salt and white pepper. Cover, remove from heat and set aside for 5 to 10 minutes so flavors blend. Add sherry before serving.

Miss Sadie: *"Now, She-Crab Soup is nothin' to snub your nose at. It comes from around Charleston, there in the Low Country. Some of the best cooks in the world live over there and they know just what to do with those sweet, little female crabs. If you die before you get to the Low Country to eat some She-Crab Soup, then you better make it to Heaven cause they serve it ever'day there."*

Everybody's Seafood Gumbo

¼ cup (½ stick) butter
4 tablespoons flour
2 quarts water
1½ to 2 pounds okra, sliced
6 firm tomatoes
½ cup minced onion
2 pounds shrimp
1 pound crabmeat
1 pound fish filets
1 pint fresh oysters with liquor
Rice

In heavy skillet melt butter and add flour. Stir well over medium heat to make smooth, paste-like roux. Add water, okra, tomatoes and onion and cook on low for 45 minutes.

Wash, clean and peel shrimp. Flake crabmeat and remove any pieces of shell. Remove all bones and skin from fish. When roux is rich brown color, add salt, black pepper and cayenne pepper and mix well. Add all seafood and cook on medium low for 30 minutes or until desired consistency. Serve over rice.

> *"Beaufort Town" was a seaport that was established in 1722. It had the right to collect customs. It was also called "Fish Town" in the 1700's after Blackbeard frequented the coast.*

Pirate Stew

If you can open cans, you can make this stew. Don't let the number of ingredients get to you. Leave something out if you get tired of opening cans.

3 pounds chuck steak, cubed
2 (15 ounce) cans diced tomatoes
4 (16 ounce) cans V-8 juice
1 (28 ounce) can green beans
2 (15 ounce) cans field peas with snaps
2 (15 ounce) cans sliced squash
2 (16 ounce) cans green peas
2 (14 ounce) cans cut okra
2 (15 ounce) packages frozen lima beans
3 (16 ounce) packages frozen cut yellow corn
1 (16 ounce) package frozen white corn
3 pounds onion, peeled, diced
4 pounds potatoes, cubed
1 quart water
Seasoned salt
Rosemary
Bay leaf
Curry powder
Black pepper
Thyme

Cube steak and brown in oil in bottom of soup pot. Add vegetables and season to taste with remaining ingredients. Simmer all day. Remove excess fat before serving.

Tip: This recipe makes enough for several meals so freeze some for later.

Wild Rabbit Stew

1 dressed rabbit, cut up
½ cup (1 stick) butter
2 garlic cloves, minced
1 medium onion, sliced
½ cup oil
1 (8 ounce) can tomato juice
¼ cup white vinegar
¼ cup green olives, sliced
10 drops hot sauce
½ teaspoon salt
5 medium potatoes, peeled, sliced
1 cup sherry

In Dutch oven or heavy skillet, brown rabbit in butter. Add all ingredients except potatoes and sherry. Bring mixture to boil, reduce heat and simmer for 1 hour.

Add potatoes and sherry and continue to cook another 10 minutes.

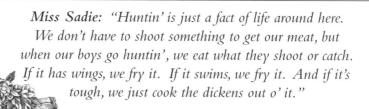

Miss Sadie: *"Huntin' is just a fact of life around here. We don't have to shoot something to get our meat, but when our boys go huntin', we eat what they shoot or catch. If it has wings, we fry it. If it swims, we fry it. And if it's tough, we just cook the dickens out o' it."*

Sister's Brunswick Stew

*This signature southern dish takes longer than most dishes,
but it is so worth it. Cook meat one day and put stew
together the next day. You'll have enough to freeze and serve
for several meals. It makes an excellent one-dish meal.*

1 (4 pound) boneless pork loin
4 to 6 chicken fryers or 6 pounds boneless, skinless
chicken pieces
9 medium potatoes, quartered
6 (28 ounce) cans stewed, diced tomatoes
2 teaspoons sugar
Salt and pepper to taste
½ medium onion, chopped
3 (16 ounce) packages frozen butterbeans, thawed
4 (16 ounce) packages frozen sweet corn, thawed

Cut pork and chicken into bite-size pieces. Cover with water and
cook very slowly until firm. Remove any bones and skin. Skim
off excess fat.

Return meat to broth, add potatoes and cook on medium. When
done, mash potatoes to thicken broth. Add tomatoes, sugar, salt
and pepper and cook until soupy. Add onion and butterbeans.
Cook on low and stir frequently.

Add corn last because it may stick to bottom of pan. Cook over
low heat until butterbeans and corn are done. (Keep scraping
bottom of pan to prevent sticking.)

---

*Miss Sadie: "There are lots o' variations on this recipe.
Ever'body's gonna' give ya' their opinion for sure."*

Frogmore Stew

Frogmore Stew originates in South Carolina's Low Country and dates back many years. According to one story passed down through the years, an old fisherman gathered up whatever he could find to put in a stew. Other stories credit specific people on St. Helena Island with the invention, but there's no disagreement to the fact that Frogmore Stew is a combination of sausage, seafood and corn. Here's one version of the famous dish.

¼ cup Old Bay seafood seasoning
3 pounds smoked link sausage, sliced
3 onions, peeled, chopped
1 lemon, sliced, seeded
Salt and pepper
6 ears corn, broken in half
½ cup (1 stick) butter
3 pounds unpeeled large shrimp
Cocktail sauce

In large pot, add about 2 gallons of water, seasoning, sausage, onions, lemon, salt and pepper. Bring to boil. Simmer uncovered for 45 minutes.

Add butter, corn and cook for 10 minutes. Add shrimp and cook for 5 more minutes. Drain. Remove with slotted spoon to serving platter. Serve with cocktail sauce.

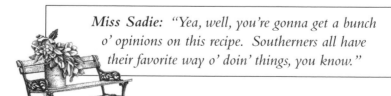

Miss Sadie: *"Yea, well, you're gonna get a bunch o' opinions on this recipe. Southerners all have their favorite way o' doin' things, you know."*

Clam Chowder

This is so good you may want to double it.

3 large potatoes
2 medium onions
3 slices bacon
1 bottle clam juice
1 pound fresh clams or 2 (6 ounce) cans minced clams
Pepper and salt to taste
1 tablespoon Worcestershire sauce
2 tablespoons cornmeal

Dice potatoes and onions, place in pot with enough water and cook until soft. While potatoes cook, fry bacon crisp enough to crumble. Save bacon drippings and add to potato mixture along with crumbled bacon. Simmer mixture for 1 minute.

Add clams, clam juice, salt, pepper and Worcestershire sauce. Thicken with cornmeal, but stir constantly so it will not be lumpy. Serve for lunch or as preface to full meal.

Tip: Serve this immediately. It won't freeze.

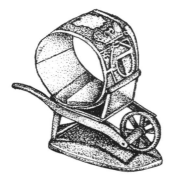

Marinated Cucumbers

1 cup vinegar
½ cup sugar
1 tablespoon chives
½ teaspoon salt
6 cucumbers, peeled

In large measuring cup, combine vinegar, sugar, chives and salt.
Slice cucumbers about ⅓-inch thick and place in large bowl.
Pour marinade over cucumbers, cover and chill.

Carrot Salad Supreme

2 (3 ounce) packages lemon gelatin
2 cups boiling water
1 tablespoon vinegar or lemon juice
½ teaspoon salt
1 (20 ounce) can crushed pineapple with juice
1 cup grated carrots
1 cup grated sharp cheddar cheese
¾ cup chopped pecans

Dissolve gelatin in boiling water and add vinegar and salt. Chill
slightly. Drain pineapple and add enough water to juice to equal
2 cups.

Fold in cheese, carrot, pineapple and pecans. Pour into mold
rinsed in cold water and chill until firm. Unmold on platter and
serve plain or use dressing of two-thirds mayonnaise and one-third
sour cream.

Fresh Okra Salad

Fresh okra
Vinaigrette salad dressing

Wash okra and cut off ends. Add okra to saucepan with boiling, salted water. Cook just until almost tender. Drain and toss with your favorite salad dressing.

Traditional Coleslaw

½ cup sugar
½ cup vinegar
¼ cup milk
1 to 2 cups mayonnaise
Salt and pepper to taste
1 large head cabbage
1 to 2 carrots, grated, optional

In mixing bowl, combine sugar, vinegar, milk and just enough mayonnaise to make dressing consistency. Add salt and pepper to taste.

Peel outside leaves of cabbage, wash and chop finely in food processor or on grater. Grate carrots and mix with cabbage. Mix dressing and cabbage well, cover bowl and refrigerate.

Spinach-Salad Mold

1 (10 ounce) package frozen chopped spinach, thawed
1 (3 ounce) package lemon or lime gelatin
¾ cup boiling water
1 cup mayonnaise
1 cup cottage cheese, drained
⅓ cup diced celery
⅓ cup diced onion

Squeeze liquid from thawed spinach and set aside. Do not cook.

Dissolve gelatin in boiling water and set aside to cool. Combine spinach and remaining ingredients with gelatin and mix well. Pour mixture into ring mold and chill until firm. Unmold and garnish as desired to serve.

Williamsburg Salad

2 (1 ounce) packages unflavored gelatin
½ cup water
1 cup boiling water
½ cup vinegar
½ teaspoon salt
1 cup sugar
1 cup chopped pecans
1 cup chopped sweet pickle relish
1 cup crushed pineapple, drained with ½ cup juice
1 cup sliced stuffed olives

Soften gelatin in water and dissolve in boiling water. Add vinegar, salt, sugar, pecans, relish, pineapple, ½ cup pineapple juice and olives. Chill and pour into molds.

Savory Layer Salad

Make this salad the day before you need it.

2½ cups mayonnaise
1 pint sour cream
Worcestershire sauce to taste
Hot sauce to taste
Salt and pepper to taste
¼ cup lemon juice
1 package fresh spinach, torn in pieces
1 head iceberg lettuce, torn in pieces
1 cup (or less) sliced green onions
1 pound bacon, cooked, crumbled
6 hard-boiled eggs, sliced
1 (10 ounce) package frozen green peas, thawed
1½ cups grated Swiss cheese

In bowl, combine mayonnaise, sour cream, Worcestershire sauce, hot sauce, salt, pepper and lemon juice and mix well. Wash and prepare salad greens and onion and combine with crumbled bacon.

Pour salad mixture into 9 x 13-inch baking dish and spread mayonnaise mixture evenly over top of salad. Layer eggs and thawed peas. Top with grated Swiss cheese. Cover and chill for 24 hours.

Perfect Potato Salad

3 medium potatoes
1 teaspoon sugar
1 teaspoon vinegar
½ cup sliced celery
⅓ cup finely chopped onion
¼ cup chopped sweet pickles
1 teaspoon salt
1 teaspoon celery seed
¾ cup mayonnaise or salad dressing
2 hard-boiled eggs, sliced

In covered pan, cook whole potatoes in boiling, salted water for 25 minutes or until tender. Drain well and peel. Cut potatoes in quarters and slice ¼-inch thick.

Add remaining ingredients except mayonnaise and eggs. Stir mixture. Fold in mayonnaise then carefully fold in egg slices. Cover and chill thoroughly.

Rice came to the South by way of a storm-ravaged, merchant ship sailing from Madagascar and reaching the port of Charleston for safe haven. As a gift to the people, the ship's captain gave a local planter "Golden Seed Rice" and by 1700, rice was a major crop in the colonies. The success of the crop gave rise to the name "Carolina Gold Rice".

The Mason-Dixon Line was the boundary between Pennsylvania and Maryland surveyed in the 1760's to settle a dispute between the colonies. Over time it has come to mean the division of the North and the South.

Rice Salad

2 (6 ounce) packages chicken Rice-a-Roni
¾ cup green pepper, chopped, optional
8 green onions, chopped
16 stuffed or ripe olives, sliced
2 (6 ounce) jars marinated artichoke hearts, cut,
reserve juice
½ to ⅔ cup mayonnaise
½ teaspoon curry powder, optional

Cook rice according to package directions, but omit butter. Cool.

Add pepper, olives, onions and drained artichokes. Save marinade
and mix with mayonnaise and curry powder. Add to rice mixture
with shrimp and press into mold. Chill.

Frozen Cranberry-Fruit Salad

1 (8 ounce) package cream cheese, softened
½ cup powdered sugar
1 tablespoon lemon juice
½ cup mayonnaise
1 (16 ounce) can whole cranberry sauce
1 cup whipped topping

In bowl, combine cream cheese, confectioners' sugar, lemon
juice and mayonnaise and blend well. Add cranberry sauce and
whipped topping to cream cheese mixture and turn into
8 x 8-inch pan. Chill. Cut into squares before serving.

Dreamy Blueberry Salad

1 (8 ounce) can crushed pineapple with juice
2 (3 ounce) packages raspberry gelatin
1 (16 ounce) can blueberries, drained

Add enough water to pineapple juice to make 2 cups. Pour into saucepan and bring to boil. Pour hot liquid over gelatin and dissolve.

Chill until mixture is consistency of egg whites. Mix blueberries and pineapple into gelatin and chill again.

Topping:

1 (8 ounce) package cream cheese
1 (8 ounce) carton sour cream
½ cup sugar
Chopped pecans

Use mixer to blend cream cheese, sour cream and sugar. Stir in pecans. Spread over congealed salad.

Strawberry Salad

2 (3 ounce) packages strawberry gelatin
1⅔ cups boiling water
2 (10 ounce) packages frozen strawberries
1 cup crushed pineapple with juice
1 cup chopped walnuts
2 bananas, sliced, optional
1(16 ounce) carton sour cream

Dissolve gelatin in boiling water. Add frozen strawberries, remove from heat and stir occasionally until strawberries thaw.

Add crushed pineapple, nuts and bananas, if desired. Pour half mixture into 8 x 8-inch or 9 x 9-inch pan and chill for 1 hour 30 minutes or until firm. Spread sour cream over firm mixture and pour remaining mixture over top. Chill until set.

Tip: If you desire, substitute pecans for walnuts and add 2 ripe sliced bananas.

A native wild strawberry grown on the eastern coast called Fragaria Virginiana was the start of today's strawberries grown primarily in California. Cultivation of the wild Virginia strawberry started sometime in the 1600's by Native Americans who introduced them to the colonists.

St. Pat's Pear Salad

1 (10 ounce) jar mint jelly
½ cup pear juice
1 (20 ounce) can pear halves with juice
Green food coloring
Bibb lettuce
Salad dressing
Mint leaves

Combine mint jelly and pear juice in saucepan over low heat.
Add drops of green food coloring. Place 8 pear halves in melted
jelly and set aside. Baste occasionally until pears turn light green
in color. Drain pears. Arrange two pear halves with cut side up
on individual salad plates over lettuce. Fill pears with spoonful
favorite salad dressing and garnish with mint leaves.

Thanksgiving's Berry Salad

A grand accompaniment with turkey or chicken salad!

1 (1 ounce) package unflavored gelatin
¼ cup cold water
1 (6 ounce) package raspberry or cherry gelatin
1¼ cups water
1 (15 ounce) can crushed pineapple with juice
1 (14 ounce) jar cranberry-orange relish
1 cup chopped pecans

Dissolve unflavored gelatin in ¼ cup cold water. Dissolve flavored
gelatin in 1¼ cups boiling water. Mix remaining ingredients and
pour into 9 x 13-inch pan or 2-quart mold.
Chill until set.

Chicken Salad Surprise

*Delicious recipe with sliced fresh fruit such as apples
and bananas or natural cheddar or Havarti cheese.*

2½ cups chicken, cooked, diced
½ cup diced celery
½ cup diced, unpeeled apple
½ cup blanched, slivered almonds, toasted
1 small onion, minced
⅓ cup mayonnaise
1 teaspoon lemon juice
½ teaspoon salt
⅛ teaspoon pepper
1 to 2 teaspoons curry powder

Mix chicken, celery, apple, almonds and onion in bowl. Combine
mayonnaise with lemon juice, pepper, salt and curry. Stir into
chicken mixture. Serve on crisp lettuce leaves, whole-wheat toast
or as a sandwich.

---

*Alabama is home to the world's largest space
attraction and home of the U.S. Space Camp.*

*Alabama workers built the first rocket
to place humans on the moon.*

Congealed Chicken Salad

*This recipe is a great luncheon dish with asparagus and baby beets
or pickled peaches. It can be made several days before you need it.*

2 (1 ounce) packages unflavored gelatin
½ cup water
1½ cups chicken broth
1 cup finely diced celery
1 small onion, finely diced
1 (8 ounce) can baby green peas, drained
½ cup chopped nuts
3 (or more) cups diced chicken
4 hard-boiled eggs, chopped
3 tablespoons chopped sweet pickles
1 (2 ounce) jar chopped pimientos
1 cup mayonnaise

Dissolve gelatin in cold water and pour in hot chicken broth.
Combine remaining ingredients. Place mixture in flat casserole or
in 15 individual molds. Chill.

Alabama residents are called Alabamians or Alabamans.
Arkansas residents are called Arkansans.
Georgia residents are called Georgians.
Kentucky residents are called Kentuckians.
Maryland residents are called Marylanders.
Mississippi residents are called Mississippians.

Hot Chicken Salad

4 cups diced, cooked, cold chicken
2 cups chopped celery
4 hard-boiled eggs, diced
2 tablespoons finely minced onions
1 teaspoon salt
2 tablespoons lemon juice
¾ cup mayonnaise
¾ cup condensed cream of chicken soup
1 cup grated cheese
1½ cups crushed potato chips
⅔ cup toasted, finely chopped almonds

Preheat oven to 400°. In bowl, combine chicken, celery, eggs, onion, salt, lemon juice, mayonnaise and soup and mix well. Pour into 9 x 13-inch baking dish.

Combine cheese, potato chips and almonds and spread over top. Cover and chill overnight. When ready to bake, remove casserole from refrigerator and bake for 20 to 25 minutes.

North Carolina residents are called North Carolinians.
South Carolina residents are called South Carolinians.
Tennessee residents are called Tennesseans.
Virginia residents are called Virginians.
West Virginia residents are called West Virginians.

Shrimp Salad Mold

2 (1 ounce) packages unflavored gelatin
¼ cup cold water
1 (10 ounce) can tomato soup, heated
¼ cup chopped onion
¼ cup chopped green pepper
1 tablespoon lemon juice
¼ teaspoon salt
1 (8 ounce) package cream cheese, softened
1 cup mayonnaise
1 cup chopped celery
2 cups cooked, shelled, veined, bite-size shrimp

Dissolve gelatin in cold water and add to heated soup. In blender, puree onion, green pepper, lemon juice and salt and add to soup mixture.

Using mixer, blend mayonnaise and cream cheese until smooth. Add to soup mixture. Stir in celery and shrimp. Pour into 9-inch mold and chill.

Washington, Arkansas was founded in 1824 and was a popular stop for travelers headed for Texas on the Southwest Trail. Sam Houston, Davy Crockett and Jim Bowie traveled through Washington on their way to Texas. A local blacksmith, James Black, is said to have crafted the legendary Bowie knife for Jim Bowie in his shop in Washington.

Butter-Melting Breads, Fruity Jams and Preserves

Angel Biscuits

3 packages yeast
⅓ cup warm water
5 cups flour
⅓ cup sugar
1 cup shortening
2 cups buttermilk

Preheat oven to 425°. Dissolve yeast in warm water and set aside. In bowl, combine flour and sugar and cut in shortening. Add buttermilk and yeast and stir well. Chill. Use dough as needed.

On floured board or wax paper, pat out dough. Using biscuit cutter, cut out biscuits and place on sprayed baking pan. Let rise in warm place 2 to 3 hours. Bake for 12 minutes or until brown. Dough should last about 10 days.

Luncheon Muffins

1 cup (2 sticks) butter, softened
2 cups flour
1 (8 ounce) carton sour cream

Preheat oven to 350°. In bowl, combine all ingredients and mix well. Pour mixture into sprayed muffin tins and bake for 20 to 25 minutes.

Baked Asparagus Rolls

¾ cup (1½ sticks) butter, softened, divided
½ cup gorgonzola cheese, crumbled
14 slices bread, thin-sliced
1 (15 ounce) can asparagus spears
Grated parmesan cheese

In bowl, cream ½ cup (1 stick) butter and gorgonzola cheese. Remove crusts from bread slices and roll each slice flat with rolling pin. Spread cheese mixture on bread.

Drain asparagus on paper towels. Place 1 spear on bread and roll in jellyroll fashion. Place rolls side by side on baking sheet with seam down. Melt remaining butter and drizzle over rolls.

Sprinkle generously with parmesan cheese and bake at 350° for 15 to 20 minutes or until crisp and brown. Cut in thirds and serve hot.

Tip: Make the day before and store in refrigerator. Wait until baking time before sprinkling remaining butter and parmesan cheese.

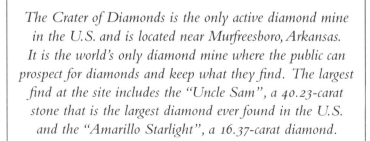

The Crater of Diamonds is the only active diamond mine in the U.S. and is located near Murfreesboro, Arkansas. It is the world's only diamond mine where the public can prospect for diamonds and keep what they find. The largest find at the site includes the "Uncle Sam", a 40.23-carat stone that is the largest diamond ever found in the U.S. and the "Amarillo Starlight", a 16.37-carat diamond.

Rich Dinner Rolls

1 cup milk
¼ cup sugar
1 teaspoon salt
¼ cup (½ stick) butter, softened
½ cup warm water
2 packages yeast or yeast cakes
2 eggs, beaten
5¼ cups unsifted flour, divided

Preheat oven to 375°. In saucepan over low heat, scald milk. Stir in sugar, salt and butter. Remove from heat and cool to lukewarm. Measure warm water into large warm bowl, sprinkle or crumble in yeast and stir until it dissolves. Add lukewarm milk mixture, eggs and 2 cups flour. Beat until smooth.

Stir in enough remaining flour to make soft dough and turn out onto lightly floured board. Knead for 8 to 10 minutes or until smooth and elastic. Place in greased bowl and turn to grease top. Cover and let rise in warm place (free from draft) for 30 minutes or until doubled in bulk.

Punch down and divide dough into 3 equal pieces. Form each piece into 9-inch roll. Cut into 9 equal pieces and form into smooth balls. Place in 3 greased, round cake pans. Cover and let rise for 30 minutes or until doubled in bulk. Brush lightly with melted butter and bake for 15 to 20 minutes.

The Georgia State Capitol, under construction
from 1883 to 1889, was dedicated as a
National Historic Landmark in 1977.

Buttermilk-Refrigerator Rolls

3 packages dry yeast
4 tablespoons warm water
5 cups flour
¼ cup sugar
¾ cup shortening, melted
2 cups buttermilk

Preheat oven to 425°. Dissolve yeast in warm water and set aside. In bowl, combine flour, sugar and melted shortening. Add buttermilk and yeast mixture and mix thoroughly by hand. Add more flour if needed. Cover and chill. Use dough as needed.

About 1 hour, 30 minutes before baking, roll dough pieces into 1-inch balls and place in muffin tin. Prepare as many rolls as needed and chill remaining dough. Cover rolls and let rise in warm place for 1 hour before baking. Bake for 12 minutes or until brown. Dough will last 10 days in plastic container.

Miss Sadie: *"Honey, if you don't keep buttermilk in your ice box, just get out 1 cup of milk and put 1 tablespoon of lemon juice or vinegar in there. Leave it alone for 10 minutes and you've got buttermilk. But honey, have you tried a big ole, cold glass of buttermilk? Hmm, Hmm!"*

Banana-Nut Bread

½ cup (1 stick) butter
1 cup sugar
2 eggs
2 cups flour
1 teaspoon baking soda
1 teaspoon cinnamon
4 ripe bananas
1 cup chopped pecans

Preheat oven to 350°. In bowl, cream butter and sugar and add eggs one at a time. Stir vigorously.

In separate bowl, combine flour, baking soda and cinnamon and stir into butter mixture a little at a time. Mash bananas and add to mixture. Stir well and add nuts. Pour into sprayed loaf pan and bake for 50 to 60 minutes.

"No Need to Knead" Rolls

2 cups lukewarm water
2 packages dry yeast
1½ teaspoons salt
1 egg
¼ cup shortening
6½ cups flour

Preheat oven to 400°. In bowl, combine all ingredients, mix well and shape into rolls. Place rolls in sprayed round cake pans.

Cover and let rise for 1 hour 30 minutes to 2 hours. Bake rolls for 15 to 20 minutes.

Christmas Cranberry Bread

2 cups flour
1 cup sugar
1½ teaspoons baking powder
½ teaspoon baking soda
1 teaspoon salt
¼ cup shortening
¾ cup orange juice
1 tablespoon grated orange rind
1 egg, well beaten
½ cup chopped nuts
1 (16 ounce) can whole cranberry sauce

Preheat oven to 350°. Sift flour, sugar, baking powder, soda and salt into bowl. Cut in shortening until mixture resembles coarse cornmeal.

In separate bowl, combine orange juice, grated rind and egg and pour into dry ingredients. Mix just enough to dampen and fold in nuts and cranberries. Spoon mixture into sprayed loaf pan and spread corners and sides slightly higher than center.

Bake for 1 hour until crust is brown and center is done. Remove, cool and store overnight for easy slicing.

Indians lived in Kentucky as long ago as 13,000 years. When European settlers came to the territory, they brought diseases that almost wiped out the native population. In the 1750's and 1760's, settlers came to the territory after hearing stories of enough game and land for everyone. The first permanent settlements were established in the 1770's and one, established by Daniel Boone, was called Fort Boonesborough.

Zucchini Bread

3 eggs
2 cups sugar
1 cup oil
2 cups grated unpeeled zucchini
3 cups all-purpose flour
1 teaspoon cinnamon
1 teaspoon salt
1 teaspoon baking powder
1 teaspoon baking soda
1 cup chopped nuts
1 teaspoon vanilla

Preheat oven to 350°. Mix all ingredients and pour into 2 sprayed loaf pans. Bake for 1 hour or until golden brown.

Cumberland Falls State Park in the Daniel Boone National Forest in Kentucky is called the "Niagara of the South". The waterfall spans more than 125 feet across and water falls more than 60 feet to the gorge below. On clear nights with a full moon, a phenomenon known as a "moon bow" can be seen through the mist of the water. This "moon bow" occurs nowhere else in the Western Hemisphere.

Pumpkin Bread

3⅓ cups flour
2 teaspoons baking soda
1½ teaspoons salt
1 teaspoon cinnamon
1 teaspoon nutmeg
4 eggs
⅔ cup water
2 cups cooked pumpkin
1 cup oil
3 cups sugar
1 cup nuts

Preheat oven to 350°. Grease 2 loaf pans and set aside. In bowl, combine flour, baking soda, salt, cinnamon and nutmeg and mix well. Add remaining ingredients to mixture and mix well.

Pour mixture into pans about ¾–full and bake for 45 minutes or until toothpick comes out clean.

Tip: Add 1 cup raisins and ¼ cup shredded coconut to above recipe.

Mammoth Cave National Park in south central Kentucky is the longest known cave system in the world. The park contains more than 52,000 acres and is home to more than 900 flowers, 21 of which are endangered or threatened.

Williamsburg Sally Lunn Bread

1 yeast cake
1 cup warm milk
½ cup (1 stick) butter
⅓ cup sugar
3 eggs, beaten
4 cups flour

Preheat oven to 350°. Put yeast cake in warm milk. In bowl, cream butter, sugar and eggs. Sift flour into yeast mixture and let rise in warm place and beat well.

Pour into well-buttered mold or 3-quart ring mold. Let rise again and bake for 45 minutes or until done. Serve hot.

The first representative assembly was
founded in Virginia in 1619.

Southern Spoon Bread

3 eggs, divided
3 cups milk
1 cup white cornmeal
1 teaspoon butter, melted
1 teaspoon sugar
1 teaspoon salt

Preheat oven to 350°. Grease 9 x 9-inch baking dish and set aside. Separate eggs and beat yolks. Beat egg whites until stiff in separate bowl. Set aside.

Scald milk in top of double boiler, add cornmeal gradually and cook 5 minutes. Stir until very smooth. Cool slightly and add butter, sugar and salt.

Add egg yolks and fold in egg whites. Pour into prepared baking dish and bake for 45 minutes.

Many southern writers including Eudora Welty, Tennessee Williams, William Faulkner, Katherine Anne Porter, Flannery O'Connor, Thomas Wolfe and Robert Penn Warren expertly represent American literature of the 20th century.

Virginia Spoon Bread

1 cup cornmeal
1 tablespoon sugar
1 teaspoon salt
¼ cup (½ stick) butter
3 eggs
2 teaspoons baking powder
1⅓ cups milk

Preheat oven to 350°. In bowl, combine cornmeal, sugar and salt. Add 1⅓ cups boiling water and butter to mixture. Stir constantly and set aside to cool.

Beat eggs until light. Stir in eggs, baking powder and milk into batter and mix well. Pour into sprayed 2-quart baking dish and place dish in baking pan with about ½-inch water. Bake about 30 to 35 minutes or until set.

The name "Virginia" was given in honor of Elizabeth, the Virgin Queen of England.

Miss Sadie: *"Oh my, I'll never forget going to Colonial Williamsburg and eatin' at Christina Campbell's Tavern. Their spoon bread was just wonderful! You know George Washington ate there. Well, not when I was there, of course.*

Sourdough Starter and Bread

Starter:
2 cups flour
2 cups warm water
1 package yeast

Dissolve yeast in warm water. Add flour and mix well. Use only glass bowl for mixing. Do not leave metal utensils in starter. Place starter in warm place overnight. Next morning, cover container and chill. Use only glass container to store starter. Chill starter when not in use and keep covered.

Every 5 days add and stir into starter:

1 cup milk
¼ cup sugar
1 cup flour, unsifted

Do not use starter on day it is fed. Always keep at least 2 cups mixture in container. Starter may be fed more frequently than every 5 days.

Sour Dough Bread:

2 cups flour, unsifted
1 tablespoon baking powder
1 teaspoon salt
2 tablespoons sugar
1 egg
2 cups Sour Dough Starter

Preheat oven to 350°. Mix dry ingredients. Add egg and starter and mix well. Turn into greased loaf pan. Place in warm place and allow to double in bulk. Bake for 30 to 35 minutes.

Cook's Best Cornbread

This is moist, much like spoon bread. It's also very good reheated and great with maple syrup.

2 eggs
1 (8 ounce) carton sour cream
½ cup salad oil
1 (8 ounce) can cream-style corn
1 cup cornmeal
3 teaspoons baking powder
1½ teaspoons salt

Preheat oven to 375°. In mixing bowl, beat eggs, sour cream, oil and corn. Blend in cornmeal, baking powder and salt.

Bake for 30 to 40 minutes in 8 x 8-inch or 9 x 9-inch pan.

Cornmeal Pone

2 cups cornmeal
2 cups cold water
1 teaspoon salt
Vegetable oil

In bowl, combine cornmeal, water and salt and stir well. Set aside for 2 minutes. Heat ¼ cup oil in flat-bottomed skillet. Drop pones by tablespoon into hot oil and fry until brown on both sides. Serve with ham slices or vegetable meal.

Eastern North Carolina Cornbread

1 cup cornmeal
½ cup flour
2 teaspoons baking powder
1 teaspoon salt
2 teaspoons sugar
1 cup milk
2 eggs
½ cup shortening

Preheat oven to 400°. Grease baking pan or muffin tins.

Sift cornmeal, flour, baking powder, salt and sugar into bowl. Stir in milk and add eggs, one at a time. Add melted shortening. Pour into prepared baking pan and bake for 20 to 25 minutes.

Virginia Dare was the 1st American-born child in 1587 in Roanoke, North Carolina. Her birth is commemorated in "The Lost Colony" outdoor drama run in Albemarle. The first year run, it was so successful that is has played ever since, nearly 60 consecutive summers.

Miss Sadie: *"In the South you better know how to make good cornbread. Bad cornbread is against the law."*

Cornbread Muffins or Squares

1¼ cups cornmeal
¾ cup flour, sifted
3 teaspoons baking powder
1 teaspoon salt
1 egg
⅓ cup salad oil
⅔ cup milk

Preheat oven to 400°. In bowl, combine cornmeal, flour, baking powder and salt. In separate bowl, combine egg, oil and milk. Combine liquid and dry ingredients and mix well with spoon.

Fill 12 sprayed muffin tins ⅔ full and bake for about 25 minutes. For squares, prepare and pour into sprayed 11 x 7-inch pan.

Golden-Fried Hush Puppies

1 cup flour
¾ cup cornmeal
1 cup finely minced onion
1¼ teaspoons baking powder
Salt
Milk

In bowl, combine all ingredients except milk. Add just enough milk to moisten, but keep batter stiff.

Heat oil in deep fryer and carefully drop spoonfuls of batter into hot oil. Fry until golden brown. Remove and drain.

Southern Mint Jelly

1½ cups packed mint leaves
3¼ cups water
Green food coloring
1 box pectin
4 cups sugar
¼ cup lemon juice

Pick out and wash fresh mint leaves. Place in saucepan with water and heat to boil. Cover and steep for 10 minutes.

Strain leaves and measure 3 cups liquid. Add few drops of green food coloring and pectin and bring to boil. Add sugar and lemon juice and bring to hard–rolling boil for 1 minute. Stir constantly. Remove from heat and skim foam off top. Pour immediately into hot, sterilized jars and seal.

Hush puppies are particularly popular in the South and served with fried catfish. They are finger-shaped biscuit or muffin type bread made of cornmeal and deep-fried. Several stories are told about the origin of the name. One such story describes an African slave who threw a plateful of the cornmeal mixture to a yelping dog to get him to stop making so much noise. Because it worked, the name Hush Puppies stuck. They are also called Corn Dodgers.

Bread-And-Butter Pickles

3 medium onions, sliced
30 (6-inch) cucumbers, sliced
5 tablespoons salt
1¼ tablespoons alum
6½ cups vinegar
5 cups sugar
3 teaspoons celery seed
2½ teaspoons mustard seed
1½ teaspoons turmeric
2½ teaspoons ginger

Slice onions and cucumbers. Sprinkle salt and alum over both and let stand 1 hour. Drain in colander and set aside.

In large pot, make syrup of vinegar, sugar, celery seed, mustard seed, turmeric and ginger and bring to boil for 5 minutes. Pour drained cucumbers into syrup.

Place in hot, sterile jars immediately and seal.

Tip: Place jars in water and bring to boil before filling so they will be hot enough to seal.

Kentucky became the 15th state in 1792 and chose to be a commonwealth building the government on the common consent of the people.

Okra Pickles

1 pod hot pepper per pint jar
2 heads dill per pint jar
1 garlic clove per pint jar
5 pounds young tender okra
8 cups vinegar
1 cup water
¾ cup salt, not iodized
1 tablespoon mixed pickling spices
¼ teaspoon alum per pint jar

In sterilized jars, place dill, garlic and hot pepper. Pack in whole, washed okra. Measure pickling spices into piece of cheesecloth and tie with string for easy removal from syrup.

Heat vinegar, salt, water and spices to boil. Pour over okra to fill jars and leave ¼-inch headspace from top of jar. Add alum to each jar. Seal immediately. Let stand 8 weeks before using.

Abraham Lincoln and Jefferson Davis, President of the Confederacy, were born in log cabins within one year and 100 miles of each other in south-central Kentucky.

Green Tomato Pickles

7 pounds green tomatoes
2 gallons water
3 cups pickling lime
5 pounds sugar
3 pints vinegar
1 tablespoon ground cloves
1 tablespoon ground ginger
1 tablespoon ground allspice
1 tablespoon celery seed
1 tablespoon ground mace
1 tablespoon ground cinnamon

Slice green tomatoes, but do not slice too thin. Dissolve lime in water, pour over tomatoes and soak for 24 hours. Stir often.

Wash tomatoes in fresh water and soak in fresh water for 4 hours, but change water every hour. Boil sugar, vinegar, spices, pour over tomatoes and let stand overnight.

Next day, boil for 1 hour. Seal in hot, sterilized jars.

*Thomas Jefferson raised tomatoes in the 1780's
and helped to spread their popularity.*

Watermelon Preserves

2 pounds watermelon rind, peeled, cubed
¼ cup pickling salt, not iodized
6 cups water, divided
1 teaspoon powdered alum
2 cups white vinegar
4 cups sugar
1 lemon, thinly sliced
1 stick cinnamon
12 whole cloves
1 teaspoon allspice

(When peeling watermelon rind be sure to leave some of pink meat on.)

Make brine with salt, 4 cups water and alum. Soak rind in mixture overnight. Drain, rinse and cook slowly in water until barely tender. Do not overcook or preserves will be too soft. Drain.

Bring to boil 2 cups water, vinegar, sugar, lemon and spices tied in cloth bag. Remove spice bag and pour hot syrup over rind. Let stand overnight.

Drain and reheat syrup for 3 mornings and pour over rind. On fourth morning, drain and reheat syrup and pour over rind packed in sterilized pint or half-pint jars. Seal.

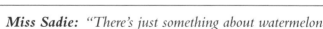

Miss Sadie: *"There's just something about watermelon preserves that reminds me of my youth. Life was good."*

Chow Chow

A delicious recipe to serve with meats and beans!

2 large heads cabbage
4 teaspoons salt
1½ pounds sweet green peppers, chopped
4 sweet red bell peppers, chopped
4 medium green tomatoes, chopped
4 medium onions, chopped
1½ pints vinegar
½ cup water
4½ teaspoons salt
3 cups sugar

Chop cabbage and add 4 teaspoons salt. Working with your hands, mix and squeeze until a bit of juice comes from cabbage.

Add chopped peppers and tomatoes. Work a bit more and add chopped onions. Make syrup of vinegar, water, salt and sugar. Place chopped vegetable ingredients into cold syrup and bring to rolling boil.

Cook for 5 minutes after boil begins. Begin to put into hot, sterile jars from center of pot. Do NOT cook too long or syrup will cook away. Seal.

> **Miss Sadie**: *"Now I need to tell ya'll about 'chow chow'. If ya'll have been so mistreated that ya'll never tasted chow chow, bless your hearts. We just put it on everything...black-eyed peas, lots o' vegetables and lots o' meat. Why, it's practically a side dish in the South."*

Fresh Veggies
Hot Casseroles
and
Fabulous Sides

Broccoli Casserole

2 (16 ounce) packages frozen broccoli spears
2 (10 ounce) cans cream of chicken soup
1 cup mayonnaise
4 teaspoons lemon juice
1 cup crushed herb dressing
4 tablespoons (½ stick) butter
1 (8 ounce) package grated, sharp cheddar cheese

Preheat oven to 350°. Cook broccoli according to package directions. Cut cooked broccoli into bite-size pieces and arrange in 9 x 13-inch glass casserole dish.

Combine soup with mayonnaise and lemon juice and pour over broccoli. Brown crushed herb dressing in butter and layer over top of casserole. Sprinkle grated cheese on top and bake for 20 to 30 minutes until bubbly.

Nineteen flags have flown over Georgia since its beginning as a territory claimed by Ferdinand and Isabella in 1474.

Skillet Cabbage

5 cups chopped cabbage
2 large onions, sliced
1 green pepper, chopped
2 tomatoes, chopped
1 tablespoon sugar
⅓ cup vegetable oil
1 teaspoon salt
½ teaspoon black pepper

Combine all ingredients in heavy skillet and cook over medium
heat for 5 to 7 minutes or until tender.

Cabbage Casserole

1 head of cabbage
1 (10 ounce) can cream of celery soup
1 (10 ounce) package grated cheddar cheese

Preheat oven to 325°. Cut up cabbage and layer in 8 x 11-inch
baking dish with celery soup and grated cheddar cheese. Bake for
35 minutes. Remove from oven and serve immediately.

Fried Fresh Corn

8 to 10 ears fresh corn
¼ cup (½ stick) butter
½ cup whipping cream
Salt and pepper
1 teaspoon sugar

With sharp knife, slit kernel rows in half. Cut off top half of corn kernels into bowl. Once kernels are cut off, tilt cob into bowl to scrape remaining juice from kernels. (Position knife at an angle to scrape corn juice off cob.)

In heavy skillet, heat butter and add corn. Stir rapidly until corn milk is thick, add cream and stir. Mix in salt, pepper and sugar. Cook mixture on low heat for 8 to 10 minutes or until mixture is thick. Serve immediately.

On April 25, 1866, a year after the Civil War, ladies of Columbus, Mississippi decorated confederate and union soldiers' graves at Friendship Cemetery with bouquets of flowers. It has since been called "Where Flowers Healed a Nation". Their gesture resulted in what we now know as Memorial Day, celebrated annually in observance of fallen war heroes.

Miss Sadie: *"Oh, honey. You haven't lived until you've eaten this fried corn! I guess if you're on one of those fancy diets, you could use sweet milk instead of whipping cream. But, my goodness, it's just so good with that heavy cream."*

Corn Fritters

¾ cup flour
1 teaspoon baking powder
½ teaspoon salt
1 tablespoon sugar
1 egg, well beaten
2 tablespoons milk
1 (12 ounce) can mexicorn, drained
Hot fat

Sift flour, baking powder, salt and sugar into bowl. In separate bowl, combine egg, milk and corn and add to flour mixture. Beat quickly and thoroughly.

Drop batter by tablespoonfuls into deep fat at 360° temperature. Fry fritters a few at a time until golden brown.

Captain Isaac Ross, who owned a plantation in Lorman, Mississippi, freed his slaves in 1834 and made arrangements for their return to Africa. Once there, they founded Liberia. Representatives of that country recently came back to visit Lorman and placed a stone at the Captain's grave site to commemorate his good deed.

Corn Pudding

This is so easy and good you may want to double it.

2 tablespoons flour
½ teaspoon salt
½ teaspoon white pepper
1 teaspoon sugar
3 eggs, well beaten
1 (15 ounce) and 1 (8 ounce) can whole-kernel corn, drained
¼ cup (½ stick) butter, melted
1 (16 ounce) carton half-and-half cream

Preheat oven to 325°. In small bowl, combine flour, salt, white pepper and sugar and set aside. In large bowl, add flour mixture, eggs, corn, melted butter (slightly cooled) and cream. Mix well and pour into sprayed 2-quart baking dish.

Cover and bake for 1 hour. Remove cover and continue to bake until top is a delicate brown color.

Nashville, Tennessee's Grand Ole Opry is known as the longest, continuous-running, radio program in the world. Since 1925, it has broadcast every weekend.

Parmesan Hominy

This makes a speedy side dish.

2 slices bacon, diced
2 tablespoons chopped onion
2 tablespoons chopped green pepper
1 (15 ounce) can hominy, drained
Seasoned salt to taste
Grated parmesan cheese

Fry bacon in skillet and cook just until still transparent. Add onion and pepper and cook until tender. Pour in drained hominy and season with seasoned salt. Heat thoroughly and top with parmesan cheese before serving.

Hominy was a great gift from Native Americans to colonists in the New World. Today it continues to be a side dish in the South and throughout the country.

Davy Crockett was born on the banks of Limestone Creek near Greenville, Tennessee, where a replica of his log cabin currently stands.

Mess O' Greens

A "mess of greens" usually means a big basket full or several big handfuls of collard greens. You wash 'em, boil 'em and season 'em with a little ham hock or bacon and you've got a real nice pot of greens ready to eat. You better eat some on New Year's Day too because they bring you money in the New Year.

1 mess of collard greens
Water
1 ham hock or thick-sliced bacon
1 teaspoon salt
½ teaspoon sugar

Wash greens carefully to remove all dirt and grit. (It takes some doin'.) Place in large pot and add about 1 inch water to pot.

Add ham hock or bunch of bacon and boil. Add equal parts of salt and sugar. Cook on low until greens are tender.

Miss Sadie: *"Ya'll need to know that a mess o' greens is really a couple o' big handfuls of anything leafy and green. Why, I remember when my mama would take me out in the field to pick 'poke salet'. It's the poor people's greens, you know. She showed me how to pick the smaller, young leaves because they were the only ones that tasted good."*

Supreme Green Beans

2 (15 ounce) cans French-style green beans, drained
1 (8 ounce) can sliced water chestnuts, drained
1 onion, chopped finely
2 tablespoons (¼ stick) butter
1 teaspoon salt
2 teaspoons soy sauce
⅛ teaspoon hot sauce
2 tablespoons Worcestershire sauce
1 (10 ounce) can cream of mushroom soup
1 (8 ounce) package shredded sharp cheddar cheese
1 (3 ounce) can French fried onion rings

Preheat oven to 350°. Place drained green beans and water chestnuts in 2½-quart sprayed baking dish.

In skillet, sauté onion in butter and add in salt, soy sauce, hot sauce, Worcestershire sauce, soup and cheese. Spoon mixture over green beans, cover and bake for 30 minutes. Remove cover, sprinkle onion rings over top and return to oven for 10 to 15 minutes.

Southerners have a tradition of cooking "a mess o' greens" served with black-eyed peas on New Year's Day to bring good luck and money in the new year.

Fresh String Beans

2 to 3 pounds fresh green beans
3 tablespoons bacon drippings
½ teaspoon salt
2 teaspoons dried basil, optional

Snap ends of green beans, wash and place in large saucepan. Pour about 1-inch water in pan and add bacon drippings, salt and basil. Bring to boil, reduce heat and cover. Cook over low heat for 15 to 20 minutes.

Minted Peas

½ cup water
1 teaspoon dried mint leaves
Pinch of sugar
Salt and pepper to taste
1 (10 ounce) package frozen tiny peas, thawed
Lump of butter

In saucepan, combine water, mint, sugar, salt and pepper and bring to boil. Add peas and cook for 2 to 3 minutes. Drain slightly and add butter.

> *Primary agricultural crops in Alabama include*
> *poultry, soybeans, milk, vegetables, wheat, cattle,*
> *cotton, peanuts, fruits, hogs and corn.*

Green Beans and Mushrooms

2 (16 ounce) packages frozen French style green beans
1 onion, chopped
1 cup chopped pecans, divided
1 (10 ounce) cream of mushroom soup
1 (10 ounce) cream of chicken soup
6 large, fresh mushrooms, sliced

Preheat oven to 375°. Cook green beans according to package directions and add onion. Drain and pour into sprayed 9 x 13-inch baking dish.

In saucepan, combine ½ cup pecans, both soups and mushrooms and heat but DO NOT COOK. Pour mixture over green beans and sprinkle with remaining pecans. Cover and bake for about 25 minutes.

Agriculture has always been a primary part of Mississippi's economy with farmers raising corn, rice, peanuts, pecans, sweet potatoes and sugar cane. Mississippi has always been the world's largest producer of the pond-raised catfish.

Stuffed Green Peppers

4½ sweet bell peppers, divided
1 large onion
1 rib celery
½ bunch shallots
2 cloves garlic
2 tablespoons (¼ stick) butter
2 tablespoons fresh chopped parsley
½ pound ground beef
2 or 3 slices white bread
¼ cup water
1 or 2 eggs as needed
1 carrot, grated
½ teaspoon sugar
Salt and pepper
1 cup dry, seasoned breadcrumbs

Preheat oven to 350°. Parboil 4 peppers for 3 minutes. Cut each pepper in half and cool. Finely chop remaining ½ pepper, onion, celery and shallots. Place in saucepan and sauté with garlic and butter. Add parsley and ground beef to mixture and cook until well done. Remove from heat and set aside.

Soak bread in water and 1 egg. Add bread and grated carrot to meat mixture and mix well. Add sugar, salt and pepper to taste. If mixture is too stiff, add remaining egg.

Fill bell pepper shells with meat mixture, cover with breadcrumbs and dot with butter. Bake for 30 to 40 minutes.

Creamed Peas and Mushrooms Elegant

4 slices bacon
¼ cup finely chopped onion
2 tablespoons flour
1 cup milk
¼ teaspoon salt
Dash of pepper
1 (15 ounce) can green peas, drained
1 (4 ounce) can sliced mushrooms, drained
1 (2 ounce) jar chopped pimiento
1 tablespoon butter
6 small, individual-size frozen piecrusts, cooked

In skillet, fry bacon until crisp. Remove, drain and crumble.

Add onion to drippings in skillet and sauté until tender. Pour off all but 1 tablespoon drippings. Blend in flour and add milk, salt and pepper. Cook and stir until thick. Stir in drained peas.

Saute mushrooms and pimiento in butter and add to peas. Serve in individual-size piecrusts.

Four of the first five presidents were from Virginia.

Baked Acorn Squash

3 acorn squash
Grated nutmeg or ground ginger
Salt
Freshly ground black pepper
3 teaspoons brown sugar
6 teaspoons (¾ stick) butter, divided
6 teaspoons sweet sherry, optional

Preheat oven to 325°. Split squash into halves and scoop out fiber and seeds. Sprinkle cavity of each half with nutmeg, salt, pepper, brown sugar and 1 teaspoon butter.

Bake 30 to 45 minutes or until flesh is tender. Add 1 teaspoon sherry to each cavity about 5 minutes before serving.

Ice tea is served year round in the South and is called sweet tea. Sweet tea is sweetened with sugar at the time it is brewed. South Carolina was the first and only state to produce tea and sell it commercially. In 1995, South Carolina General Assembly adopted sweet tea as the Official Hospitality Beverage for the state.

Summer Squash Casserole

½ cup (1 stick) butter
1 (8 ounce) package herb dressing
2 pounds yellow squash, sliced, cooked, drained
2 small onions, finely chopped
1 (10 ounce) can cream of chicken soup
1 (5 ounce) can sliced water chestnuts
1 (2 ounce) jar chopped pimiento, optional

Preheat oven to 350°. Melt butter and stir into dressing. Divide and place half in 8 x 12-inch baking dish. Combine squash, onions, soup, chestnuts and pimientos and pour over dressing. Cover squash with remaining dressing and bake for 30 to 40 minutes.

Battletown Inn Yellow Squash

7 small yellow squash, sliced
1 small onion, diced
2 tablespoons (¼ stick) butter
½ cup half-and-half cream
¾ cup saltine cracker crumbs, divided

Preheat oven to 350°. Boil squash in salt water until tender. Drain and mash. Grease 1½-quart baking dish and set aside.

Sauté onion in butter. Add cream and ¼ cup cracker crumbs to onion and mix with squash. Pour into baking dish, top with remaining crumbs and dot with butter. Bake 30 to 45 minutes or until top is brown.

Squash Casserole

2 pounds yellow squash
1 large yellow onion, diced
Water
1 tablespoon salt
2 cups dry, seasoned breadcrumbs, divided
3 eggs, well-beaten
1 (8 ounce) package shredded Colby and Monterrey
    Jack cheese, divided
1 (8 ounce) carton whipping cream
1 teaspoon dried basil
1 teaspoon white pepper

Preheat oven to 350°. Clean squash and slice. Place squash and onion in pot and cover with cold water. Add salt and bring to boil. Reduce heat to medium and cook about 15 minutes or until very tender. Drain well and place in large mixing bowl. Fold in half breadcrumbs, eggs, half cheese and cream and mix well. Stir in basil and white pepper.

Pour into sprayed baking dish and sprinkle with remaining breadcrumbs and cheese. Cover and bake for 3 minutes. Remove cover and return to oven for another 10 minutes or until light brown on top.

Scalloped Okra and Corn

1 (15 ounce) can cut okra, drained
¼ cup (½ stick) butter, divided
1 (15 ounce) can whole kernel corn, drained
1 (10 ounce) can cream of celery soup
1 (8 ounce) package shredded sharp cheddar cheese
1 cup dry, seasoned breadcrumbs

Preheat oven to 350°. In skillet with 2 tablespoons (¼ stick) butter, stir fry okra for 10 minutes. Place okra in sprayed 7 x 11-inch baking dish and alternate with layers of corn. Heat soup in saucepan, stir in cheese and pour over vegetables. Cover with breadcrumbs and dot with butter. Bake for 35 minutes or until breadcrumbs brown.

Okra Lovers Fried Okra

2 eggs, lightly beaten
2 tablespoons milk
¾ cup cornmeal
¼ cup flour
1 teaspoon salt
22 to 28 fresh okra pods, thinly sliced
¼ cup oil

In shallow bowl, combine eggs and milk and mix well. In separate bowl, combine cornmeal, flour and salt. Dip okra slices in egg-milk mixture and then in cornmeal mixture. Place okra in heavy skillet with oil and cook on medium to high heat until okra browns. Stir occasionally. Drain on paper towels.

Fried Green Tomatoes

1 pound green tomatoes
1 cup flour
1 to 2 tablespoons light brown sugar
½ teaspoon salt
½ teaspoon pepper
Canola oil

Cut ends off tomatoes, slice ⅓-inch thick and lay on paper towels to drain. Mix flour, brown sugar, salt and pepper in shallow bowl.

Dredge tomatoes in flour thoroughly. Heat oil and carefully place each slice in skillet. When 1 side of tomato is crispy and golden in color, turn to brown other side. Drain on paper towels and serve immediately.

Tip: If you do most of your frying in a cast-iron skillet, add chopped onion to the skillet to absorb some of the tomatoes' acid. It will protect your skillet.

Thomas Jefferson raised tomatoes in the 1780's
and helped to spread their popularity.

Baked, Stuffed Tomatoes

6 large tomatoes
¼ teaspoon salt
⅛ teaspoon pepper
½ cup finely minced shallots
½ teaspoon garlic powder
2 tablespoons fresh, chopped basil
4 tablespoons fresh, minced parsley
½ teaspoon sugar
¼ teaspoon thyme
2 cups dry, seasoned breadcrumbs
Olive oil

Preheat oven to 400°. Cut tomatoes in half and seed. Sprinkle lightly with salt and pepper. Place tomatoes in buttered, shallow baking dish.

In bowl, combine shallots, garlic powder, basil, parsley, sugar, thyme and breadcrumbs. Fill tomatoes with mixture and drizzle with olive oil. Bake for 10 to 15 minutes.

Southern-Style Onion Rings

1 cup beer (not light beer)
1 cup flour
2 large, yellow or Vidalia onions
Vegetable oil

Preheat oven to 200°. In bowl, combine beer and flour, mix well and set aside for 3 to 4 hours (this is an important step). Slice onions into rings of desired width and dip into batter. Fry in hot oil deep enough to cover rings. Remove and drain on paper towels. As you cook onions, place them on shallow baking pan lined with brown paper. Keep hot in 200° oven.

Baked Vidalia Onions

1 large Vidalia onion, per person
1 tablespoon butter, per onion
½ teaspoon salt, per onion
¼ teaspoon black pepper, per onion
1 (8 ounce) package shredded sharp cheddar cheese,
divided

Preheat oven to 350°. Remove outer skin of onions. With sharp knife, remove very thin slice from bottom or root end of onion to allow onion to sit flat. Quarter onions, almost cutting down to core but not all the way.

Insert tablespoon butter into center slit. Salt and pepper heavily and sprinkle heaping tablespoon cheese. Wrap onions individually in foil and bake for about 1 hour.

Scalloped Onions

6 yellow onions
1½ teaspoons salt, divided
¼ teaspoon black pepper
¾ cup shredded cheddar cheese
½ teaspoon dried thyme leaves
1 cup (2 sticks) butter, sliced
1 (8 ounce) carton whipping cream
1 cup dry, seasoned breadcrumbs
⅓ cup grated parmesan cheese

Preheat oven to 350°. Slice onions about 1-inch thick. Place in heavy pot with 1 inch or more of water to cover onions. Add 1 teaspoon salt and bring to boil. Reduce heat, cover and simmer 15 minutes. (Add a little more water if necessary to cover onions.)

Drain onions and place half in sprayed baking dish. Sprinkle remaining ½ teaspoon salt, pepper, cheese and thyme. Place butter slices over onions, add last layer of onion and pour cream over top. Sprinkle with breadcrumbs and parmesan cheese and bake uncovered for 35 minutes or until breadcrumbs are light brown.

In the fields around Vidalia and Glennville in southern Georgia, the granex seed produces one of the sweetest onions grown. The granex seed grown in other parts of the U.S. produces a hotter onion. What makes the onion sweet in the Vidalia area is a mystery. The Vidalia onion was designated as the Official Vegetable of Georgia in 1990.

Vidalia Onion Sandwiches

Thin white bread
Vidalia onions
Mayonnaise
Salt and pepper

Cut out bread rounds about same diameter as onions. Coat amply
with mayonnaise and top with very thin slice of onion. Sprinkle
liberally with salt and pepper. Serve cold.

Miss Sadie: *"I'll tell you a little secret. My favorite*
sandwich is as simple as can be. I cut 1 to 2 thick slices of a
big garden tomato and a couple of big slices of a Vidalia onion
(just the best in the world) and put them on some day-old
white bread. Dab a little mayonnaise on that bread and
take big ole bites. With a glass of ice-
cold, sweet tea, I'm in Heaven."

Buttered Turnips

5 medium turnips, peeled, diced
2 teaspoons sugar
1½ teaspoons salt
½ teaspoon pepper
¼ cup (½ stick) butter, melted
Salt and pepper to taste

In saucepan, combine turnips with sugar, salt and pepper and cook
until tender. Rinse well, drain thoroughly and pour into serving
dish. Add butter, mash and season to taste with more salt and
pepper.

Turnip Casserole

3 pounds turnips
¼ cup (½ stick) butter
1½ tablespoons sugar
1½ teaspoons salt
Pepper
3 eggs
1 cup dry, seasoned breadcrumbs
1½ teaspoons lemon juice

Preheat oven to 375°. Pare and cut turnips into small slices. Boil until tender, drain and mash hot turnips with butter, sugar, salt and pepper. Beat with electric mixer until ingredients blend well. Add eggs one at a time and beat until fluffy. Stir in breadcrumbs and lemon juice.

Pour into 1½-quart baking dish, cover and chill until baking time. Bake for 50 minutes.

The Tennessee nickname is "The Volunteer State" came about during the War of 1812 when volunteer soldiers from that state displayed valor fighting in the Battle of New Orleans.

Zucchini Souffle

Butter
5 to 6 zucchini (about 2½ pounds) with peel
1 teaspoon salt
⅓ cup flour
4 large eggs
1 cup heavy cream
1 cup grated Swiss cheese
1½ teaspoons salt
½ teaspoon white pepper

Preheat oven to 350°. Butter 7 x 9-inch baking dish. Boil zucchini with peel in salt water for 6 to 8 minutes. Drain well and puree in blender. Sprinkle flour on top, add remaining ingredients and mix well.

Pour into prepared baking dish and bake for 45 minutes. If not brown at end of cooking time, place under broiler for several minutes. Set aside for
10 minutes before serving.

Tip: This is really easy and you can do part of it in advance. Serve immediately and eat it all because it doesn't freeze well.

Samuel Powhatan Carter was born in Elizabethton, Tennessee and is known in American history as the only person to be both a Navy Admiral and Army General.

Hoppin' John

This recipe (field peas over rice) is a southern dish and traditional on New Year's Eve and New Year's Day. The tradition is to eat field peas or black-eyed peas for luck and collard greens for money in the New Year.

2 small onions, chopped
8 slices bacon, cut into pieces
¼ cup (½ stick) butter
1 cup cooked ham, cubed
2½ cups water
1 cup uncooked rice
3 (15 ounce) cans black-eyed peas with liquid
Cayenne pepper

In skillet, sauté onion in butter for 5 minutes and add bacon pieces. Cook until light brown. Add remaining ingredients to skillet and continue to cook over medium heat for 25 minutes.

Black-Eyed Peas

1 cup dried black-eyed peas
2 slices salt pork
1 medium onion, chopped
2 teaspoons salt
¼ teaspoon garlic powder

Wash peas and place in large pot with 6 cups hot water. Add pork, onion, salt and garlic powder. Cover, bring to slow boil and simmer over low heat for 2 hours, 30 minutes or until tender. Drain before serving.

Barbequed Baked Beans

*These are not your ordinary beans and they
are great with barbequed pork!*

1 (15 ounce) can pork and beans
1 (15 ounce) can kidney beans, drained
1 (15 ounce) can green lima beans, drained
1 large onion, chopped
1 clove garlic, minced
1 tablespoon Worcestershire sauce
1 teaspoon ground cumin
2 to 3 tablespoons strong cold coffee
¼ cup packed brown sugar
½ cup ketchup
Pinch oregano
Pinch sweet basil
Dash hot sauce
3 bacon slices

Preheat oven to 350°. Combine all ingredients in 9 x 13-inch baking dish. Place bacon slices on top. Cover with foil and bake at 350° for 1 hour.

Remove cover and continue baking for 15 more minutes.

The Francis Beidler Forest near Charleston, South Carolina, claims the largest remaining virgin stand of bald cypress and tupelo trees in the world.

Twice-Baked Potatoes

2 large baking potatoes
2 tablespoons (¼ stick) butter
2 tablespoons mayonnaise
¼ teaspoon salt
⅛ teaspoon pepper
1 tablespoon chopped chives
½ cup shredded cheddar cheese
Paprika

Preheat oven to 400°. Scrub potatoes, rub skins with oil and bake for 1 hour. Allow potatoes to cool to touch. Cut potatoes in half lengthwise, scoop out pulp and leave shells intact.

Mash pulp and combine with butter, mayonnaise, salt, pepper and chives. Mix well and stuff shells with mixture. Sprinkle with cheese and paprika and place in shallow baking dish. Bake at 375° for 20 minutes.

"Hunley's Boat" was the first submarine used in warfare. Confederates used it in 1863 in the Charleston Harbor.

Vegetables   95

Sweet Potato Souffle

3 cups cooked, mashed sweet potatoes
1 cup sugar
½ teaspoon salt
2 eggs, beaten lightly
3 tablespoons butter, melted
1 cup half-and-half cream
1 teaspoon vanilla

Topping:

⅓ cup (⅔ stick) butter
1 cup packed brown sugar
⅓ cup flour
1 cup chopped pecans
1 cup shredded coconut

Preheat oven to 350°. In bowl, combine sweet potatoes and sugar and mix well. Add salt and eggs and stir. Add butter, cream and vanilla and stir. Pour sweet potato mixture into sprayed baking dish and bake for 35 minutes. Remove from oven and set aside.

To prepare topping, melt butter and add sugar, flour, pecans and coconut. Mix well. Spread mixture over top of baked sweet potatoes, return to oven and bake for 20 additional minutes.

Sweet Potato Balls
Looks like you worked all day, but no way!

2 cups crushed corn flakes
1 cup plus 3 tablespoons packed brown sugar, divided
1 (20 ounce) can sliced pineapple, drained
1 (28 ounce) can sweet potatoes or yams
¼ teaspoon lemon extract
1 teaspoon cinnamon
¼ teaspoon nutmeg
2 tablespoons (¼ stick) butter, softened
10 red cherries

Preheat oven to 350°. Mix crushed corn flakes and 3 tablespoons brown sugar in shallow dish and set aside. Place 10 slices pineapple on sprayed baking sheet.

Drain sweet potatoes, place in bowl and mash with fork. Add 1 cup packed brown sugar, lemon extract, cinnamon, nutmeg and butter to sweet potatoes and beat with electric mixer until smooth. With hands, form 10 balls of sweet potato mixture and roll in corn flake mixture until it coats well.

Place sweet potato ball on pineapple slice and top with cherry. Chill until ready to bake. Dot with extra butter and bake for 25 minutes.

Miss Sadie: *"Sweet potatoes are just as good as they can be and good for you. They have lots of fiber and are just full of Vitamin C & E. Now take care of yourself."*

Brandied Sweet Potatoes

2½ pounds sweet potatoes
½ cup (1 stick) butter
½ cup packed light brown sugar
¼ teaspoon nutmeg
1 teaspoon cinnamon
½ teaspoon salt
½ cup brandy or sherry

Preheat oven to 375°. Grease shallow baking dish. Boil potatoes or yams in skins until soft, remove and cool. Peel and slice crosswise about 1½-inch thick.

Place in prepared baking dish and dot with butter. In bowl, combine sugar, nutmeg, cinnamon and salt and sprinkle mixture over potatoes. Pour brandy or sherry over all and bake for 30 minutes.

The sweet potato, a Southern favorite, is one of the most nutritious vegetables we have. It is fat free and cholesterol free, is full of fiber and has significant amounts of vitamin C and vitamin E. They can be baked, grilled, sautéed, fried, boiled, steamed and eaten raw in appetizers, salads, side dishes, main dishes, breads and even desserts.

Short-Cut Cornbread Dressing

2 (8 ounce) packages cornbread mix
9 biscuits or 1 recipe biscuit mix
1 small onion, chopped
2 ribs celery, chopped
2 eggs
Black pepper
2 teaspoons poultry seasoning
3 (14 ounce) cans chicken broth, divided

Prepare cornbread and biscuits according to package directions. Crumble cornbread and biscuits into large bowl. (Use a little more cornbread than biscuits.) Add onion, celery, eggs and seasonings and stir in 2½ cans broth. If mixture is not runny, add remaining broth. (If it is still not runny, add a little milk.)

Pour mixture into sprayed 9 x 13-inch baking dish and bake for 45 minutes or until golden brown.

Giblet Gravy:

2 (14 ounce) cans chicken broth, divided
2 heaping tablespoons cornstarch
Black pepper
Cooked chicken or turkey giblets, chopped
2 hard-boiled eggs, sliced

Mix ½ cup chicken broth with cornstarch in saucepan and stir until there are no lumps. Add remaining broth and heat to boil and stir constantly until broth is thick. Add three-fourths of egg slices.

Add cooked giblets and pour into gravy boat. Garnish with remaining egg slices.

Low Country Oyster Dressing

12 cups cubed, day-old bread
1 cup (2 sticks) butter
2 cups chopped celery
1½ cups chopped onion
1½ pints oysters with liquor, chopped
3 eggs, beaten
1 teaspoon salt

Place bread in large bowl and set aside. Sauté celery and onions in butter and pour into bowl with bread.

Drain liquor of oysters into small bowl. Mix chopped oysters, eggs and salt into bread mixture. Use oyster liquor and milk to moisten mixture if needed.

Oyster-Cornbread Dressing

5 cups crumbled cornbread
4 cups toasted bread pieces
1 (14 ounce) can chicken broth
1½ cups chopped onion
1⅓ cups chopped celery
1 green pepper, chopped
½ cup (1 stick) butter, plus 2 tablespoons butter
1 (16 ounce) carton raw oysters, drained, chopped
⅓ cup fresh chopped parsley
½ teaspoon sage
½ teaspoon thyme
Salt and pepper
2 eggs, beaten

Preheat oven to 350°. Soak cornbread and bread pieces in chicken broth. In saucepan, cook onion, celery and green pepper in 2 tablespoons (¼ stick) butter until tender.

Prepare oysters separately by simmering in saucepan with a little butter until edges curl. Remove from heat and drain well. Combine with breads, remaining butter and remaining ingredients.

Use dressing to stuff turkey or shape into patties. Bake patties uncovered for 30 minutes.

Brown Rice Dressing

1½ cup uncooked brown rice
1 teaspoon salt
1 teaspoon rosemary
3 cubes chicken bouillon
6 slices bacon
½ cup diced green onions
2 tablespoons (¼ stick) butter, melted
1 (8 ounce) can sliced water chestnuts

Preheat oven to 325°. In saucepan combine 3 cups water, salt, rosemary and bouillon and bring to boil. Add uncooked rice, cover and simmer
30 minutes or until all liquid absorbs into rice.

Fry bacon until crisp and crumble into small pieces. Combine bacon, green onion, butter and water chestnuts and add to rice. Mix well and place in 7 x 11-inch baking dish. Cover and bake for 15 minutes.

Rice came to the South by way of a storm-ravaged, merchant ship sailing from Madagascar and reaching the port of Charleston for safe haven. As a gift to the people, the ship's captain gave a local planter some "Golden Seed Rice" and by 1700, rice was a major crop in the colonies. The success of the crop gave rise to the name "Carolina Gold Rice".

3-Cheese Macaroni

1 (16 ounce) package macaroni
¼ cup (½ stick) butter, divided
1 (8 ounce) package longhorn cheese, cubed
1 cup cubed Swiss cheese
¼ cup grated parmesan cheese
1 tablespoon flour
Salt and pepper to taste
1½ cups milk

Preheat oven to 350°. Cook macaroni according to package directions. Drain and stir in half butter to keep macaroni from sticking together. While macaroni is still warm, mix in 3 cheeses and stir until they melt. Pour mixture into sprayed 9 x 13-inch baking dish.

In saucepan, melt remaining butter and add flour plus a little salt and pepper. Cook and stir 1 minute. Slowly add milk and stir constantly. Cook until thick and pour over macaroni cheese mixture. Bake covered for 25 minutes. Remove cover and continue to cook for 10 more minutes.

Southern Macaroni and Cheese

1 (16 ounce) package shell pasta
2 teaspoons salt
2 tablespoons (¼ stick) butter
3 eggs, beaten
1 (16 ounce) carton half-and-half cream
1 (12 ounce) package cheddar cheese, divided
⅛ teaspoon cayenne pepper

Preheat oven to 350°. Combine pasta and 2 teaspoons salt in large saucepan and cook for 6 minutes. (Pasta should be slightly uncooked.) Drain pasta and stir in butter to keep it from sticking. Transfer to sprayed 2½-quart baking dish.

In bowl, combine eggs, cream, ¾ cheese and cayenne pepper and mix well. Pour mixture over pasta and sprinkle remaining cheese over top. Cover and bake for 35 minutes. Remove cover and broil just enough to lightly brown top.

Macaroni and Cheese is probably the ultimate comfort food and may have originated in the South. In Mary Randolph's The Virginia Housewife published in 1824, there is a recipe for macaroni and cheese. We know from Thomas Jefferson's travels, that he returned from France with knowledge of macaroni and how to make it. Based on his interest in food, it is not inconceivable that he had some influence on the dish, particularly since he served it in the White House in 1802.

Grits You Will Love

2 tablespoons (¼ stick) butter
1 small onion, chopped
3 cups water
½ teaspoon salt
⅛ teaspoon cayenne pepper
1 cup quick-cooking grits
¾ cup grated cheddar cheese

Preheat oven to 350°. Melt butter in saucepan and add onion. Cook onion for 3 minutes, pour in water, salt and cayenne pepper and bring to boil. Stir in grits and cook on medium heat for 2 minutes or until thick. Stir, add in cheese and mix well.

Pour mixture into sprayed 2-quart baking dish and bake uncovered for 30 minutes or until brown on top.

Miss Sadie: *"Just so you all will understand one of the specialties of the South, I'll explain grits. We have fresh corn. We let that dry and then call it hominy. We grind up hominy and call that grits. Just think of grits as posole."*

Garlic-Seasoned Grits

1 cup uncooked grits
1 (5 ounce) roll garlic cheese
½ cup (1 stick) butter
2 eggs
Milk

Preheat oven to 350°. Cook grits in saucepan according to package directions. Add garlic cheese, butter, eggs and milk. Stir well.

Beat eggs slightly, pour into measuring cup and add enough milk to equal 1 cup. Add to grits and mix well. Pour grits mixture into sprayed baking dish and bake for 30 minutes or until light brown on top.

Grits became the Official Prepared Food of Georgia in 2002. They are made from bits of ground corn or hominy and are used as a breakfast dish or side dish.

Slap-Yo'-Mama Main Dishes

More Than Burgers Beef
Chicken Lickin' Good
Pig Pickin' Pork Galore
Coastal Fresh, Tried and True Seafood Too
Feather, Fin and Game

Stuffed Cabbage

1 large head cabbage, cored
1½ pounds lean ground beef
1 egg, beaten
3 tablespoons ketchup
⅓ cup dry, seasoned breadcrumbs
2 tablespoons dried, minced onion flakes
1 teaspoon seasoned salt
2 (15 ounce) cans Italian stewed tomatoes
¼ cup cornstarch
3 tablespoons brown sugar
2 tablespoons Worcestershire sauce

In large kettle, place head of cabbage in boiling water for 10 minutes or until outer leaves are tender. Drain well. Rinse in cold water and remove 10 large outer leaves. (To get that many large leaves, you may have to put 2 smaller leaves together to make one roll). Set aside.

Take remaining cabbage and slice or grate in slivers. Place in sprayed 9 x 13-inch baking dish. In large bowl, combine ground beef, egg, ketchup, breadcrumbs, onion flakes and seasoned salt and mix well. Place ½ cup meat mixture packed together on each cabbage leaf. Fold in sides and roll up leaf to completely enclose filling. You may have to remove thick vein from cabbage leaves for easier rolling.

Place each rolled leaf over grated cabbage. Place stewed tomatoes in large saucepan. Combine cornstarch, brown sugar and Worcestershire sauce and spoon mixture into tomatoes. Cook on high heat and stir until tomatoes thicken. Pour over cabbage rolls, cover and bake at 325° for 1 hour.

Super Beef Casserole

1½ pounds lean ground beef
1 onion, chopped
1 (15 ounce) can tomato sauce
½ teaspoon dried basil
1 (8 ounce) package medium noodles
1 (16 ounce) small-curd cottage cheese
1 (8 ounce) carton sour cream
1 cup shredded cheddar cheese

Preheat oven to 350°. In large skillet, brown beef and onion and drain. Stir in tomato sauce, basil and ample amount of salt and pepper. Stir well and simmer 25 minutes.

Cook noodles according to package directions, drain and rinse in cold water. Spoon noodles into sprayed 3-quart casserole dish. In bowl, combine cottage cheese and sour cream and spoon over noodles. Pour beef mixture over cottage cheese mixture and top with cheddar cheese. Bake for 25 to 30 minutes.

Daniel Boone is America's most famous pioneer and was responsible for much of the settlement of Kentucky. He improved the trails through Cumberland Gap in the Appalachian Mountains and led his family and settlers to establish Fort Boonesborough in 1775. He improved the trail between the Carolinas and the center of Kentucky and it became known as the Wilderness Trail.

Miracle Meatloaf

*This is really good if you make it early in
the day or a day before you serve it.*

1½ pounds ground beef
¼ cup dry, seasoned breadcrumbs
1 egg
½ teaspoon salt
2 cups mashed potatoes
2 hard-boiled eggs, chopped
⅓ cup mayonnaise
⅓ cup grated parmesan cheese
¼ cup finely chopped celery
2 tablespoons sliced green onion
Salt and pepper

Preheat oven to 350°. Combine beef, breadcrumbs, egg and salt
and mix well. Pat down beef mixture into 8 x 14-inch rectangle
on foil or wax paper.

Combine potatoes, hard-boiled eggs, mayonnaise, cheese, celery
and onion and mix lightly. Season to taste and spread potato
mixture over beef.

Begin at narrow end and roll in jellyroll fashion. Chill several
hours or overnight. Bake on rack of sprayed broiler pan for
40 to 45 minutes.

Savory Pepper Steak
This is an easy way to fix steak!

¼ cup flour
½ teaspoon salt
⅛ teaspoon black pepper
1½ pounds round steak cut ½-inch strips
¼ cup cooking oil
1 (15 ounce) can diced tomatoes
1 cup water
½ cup chopped onion
1 small clove garlic, minced
1 tablespoon dry beef bouillon
1½ teaspoons Worcestershire sauce
2 large green peppers, cut in strips
Hot, cooked rice

Combine flour, salt and black pepper and coat steak. In large skillet with hot oil, brown meat on both sides. Add drained tomatoes, water, onion, garlic and gravy base. Cover and let simmer for 1 hour, 15 minutes or until meat is tender.

Uncover and add Worcestershire sauce and green pepper strips. Cover again and simmer for 5 minutes more. Thicken gravy with mixture of flour and cold water. Serve over hot rice.

Company Steak Over Rice

1½ pounds round steak, cut into strips
2 onions, cut in ½-inch slices, separated into rings
1 (4 ounce) can sliced mushrooms, drained
1 (10 ounce) can cream of celery soup
1 (10 ounce) can beef broth
½ cup dry sherry
1 teaspoon seasoned salt
Hot, cooked rice

In large skillet, brown meat in a little oil over high heat. Add onion, reduce heat and simmer for 5 minutes. Add mushrooms, soup, broth, sherry, seasoned salt and ample amount of black pepper.

Simmer on low heat for 1 hour or until steak is tender. Stir occasionally.

Smothered-Fried Steak

6 cube steaks
Flour for dredging
Salt and pepper
Vegetable oil
1 large onion, sliced
1 can beef broth

Coat steaks well in flour heavily seasoned with salt and pepper. (Use remaining flour to thicken gravy later.)

In large skillet, heat oil and add steaks. Fry over medium to high heat until steaks brown on both sides. Add onion and sauté for 10 minutes. Stir in beef broth and can of water and break up any scrapings on bottom of pan.

Cover skillet and allow steaks to simmer in liquid over low heat for 1 hour or until tender. When ready to serve, combine remaining flour (about ¼ cup) with a little water and add to steaks and gravy. Stir and heat until gravy is thick.

The Official State Beef Barbecue Championship Cook-Off is called "Shoot the Bull Barbeque Cook-Off, and is held each year in Hawkinsville, Georgia.

Grilled Flank Steak

2 pounds flank steak
¼ cup soy sauce
⅓ cup honey
2 tablespoons cider vinegar
1½ teaspoons garlic salt
1 teaspoon ground ginger
¾ cup oil
1 small onion, finely minced

Score steak ¼-inch deep on each side and remove visible fat. In shallow bowl, combine soy sauce, honey, vinegar, garlic salt, ginger, oil and onion. Marinate steak overnight in refrigerator.

Remove steak from marinade and grill for 10 minutes on each side. Slice diagonally.

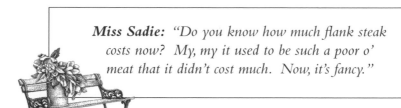

Miss Sadie: *"Do you know how much flank steak costs now? My, my it used to be such a poor o' meat that it didn't cost much. Now, it's fancy."*

Southern Country Pot Roast

1 (4 pound) lean chuck roast
2 teaspoons salt
½ teaspoon pepper
1 tablespoon paprika
2 tablespoons corn oil
1 bay leaf
2 large onions, peeled, quartered
1 (16 ounce) package baby carrots
4 large potatoes, peeled, quartered
1 (15 ounce) can tomato sauce
1 tablespoon dried parsley
1 (8 ounce) carton sour cream

Preheat oven to 350°. Sprinkle roast with salt, pepper and paprika and place in roasting pan with hot oil. Add ¾ cup water and bay leaf.

Cover and cook for 2 hours, 30 minutes. Add onions, carrots, potatoes and tomato sauce, cover and cook for 1 more hour. Remove roast from roasting pan and place on serving platter. Add parsley and sour cream to vegetables in roasting pan and stir well. Serve sauce over sliced roast and vegetables.

Pan-Fried Liver and Onions

Calf liver, sliced about ¼-inch thick
Seasoned salt
Flour
Canola oil
2 large onions

Season calf liver slices and dredge with flour in shallow bowl. Brown both sides in small amount of oil in heavy skillet.

Slice onions and separate into rings. Place rings on top of liver, cover and simmer for 20 minutes. Serve immediately.

Miss Sadie: *"I know lots of people use onions, but I like to have bacon. Fry that bacon up and cook that calf's liver in the bacon fat and child, is it good? When it's done, just crumble that bacon on top and you're in hog Heaven."*

Barbeque in the South

Even though barbeque is considered a slow method of cooking over low fire or hot coals, in the South it is considered a social event. From the beginning when Native Americans taught settlers how to cure deer, settlers taught Indians how to smoke and cure meat, primarily pork.

Barbeque (the meat) always had a way of becoming a barbeque (an event). The settlers and Indians came together for celebrations. Plantation owners had neighborly parties, church members donated the pig and women brought covered dishes. Political rallies and speech-making always drew a better crowd with barbeque (and maybe a little bourbon).

Today barbeque has grown from farmers cooking back yonder behind the barn on weekends and selling their smoked meats at road-side stands and fancy barbeque joints with chairs, red and white checked vinyl tablecloths and a smoky kind of ambience that makes it very approachable. Today barbeque is still a big event in the backyards of most Southerners.

Barbeque is a big deal in the South and most people identify the South with barbeque. The only real argument is what kind of meat and what kind of sauce goes on it. To most people in the South, pork is the only meat for barbeque. In some parts of Kentucky mutton was the preferred meat, but is now second to pork.

Barbeque in the South is a time-honored tradition and its roots are deep enough to keep it around for a long time. Just ask a Southerner what he thinks about barbeque and what is his favorite sauce. He won't mind telling you, but it will take some time.

Barbequed Brisket

1 (4 to 5 pound) trimmed beef brisket
3 ounces liquid smoke
Celery salt
Garlic salt
Onion salt
¼ cup Worcestershire sauce
Salt and pepper
¾ cup prepared barbeque sauce

Place brisket in oblong baking dish and sprinkle with liquid smoke and seasoning salts. Cover and marinate in refrigerator overnight.

Preheat oven to 275°. When ready to bake, sprinkle with Worcestershire sauce, salt and pepper. Place foil loosely over meat and cook for 5 hours. Uncover brisket and pour barbeque sauce over meat. Turn up heat to 325° and cook uncovered for 1 more hour. Remove to platter and let cool before slicing.

The World Championship Barbeque Cooking Contest is held annually in Memphis, Tennessee in May. It is billed as the largest pork barbeque cooking contest on the planet.

Barbequed Spareribs

4 pounds spareribs
1 cup firmly packed brown sugar
¼ cup ketchup
¼ cup soy sauce
1 teaspoon dry mustard
½ cup chili sauce
¼ cup rum
¼ cup Worcestershire sauce
2 cloves garlic, crushed
Pepper

Preheat oven to 375°. Place ribs in baking pan, cover with foil and bake for 30 minutes. Unwrap and drain drippings. In bowl, combine remaining ingredients and pour over ribs.

Reduce heat to 325° and bake uncovered for 1 hour, 30 minutes. Baste occasionally.

Tip: This recipe can be used for grilling also.

The Slosheye Big Pig Jig is the Official Georgia Pork Cook-Off held annually in Vienna, Georgia. It is considered the "Cadillac of barbeque contests" in the southeastern United States.

Barbeque Dry Rub

4 tablespoons paprika
2 to 3 tablespoons light brown sugar
2 tablespoons chili powder
2 tablespoons cracked black pepper
1 tablespoon cayenne pepper
1 tablespoon cumin
1 to 2 tablespoons garlic powder
1 tablespoon celery salt
1 tablespoon salt
1 to 2 teaspoons dry mustard

In bowl, mix all ingredients thoroughly. Rub mixture into meat of your choice and wrap in plastic wrap. Chill several hours or overnight.

The Magnolia Blossom Festival and World Championship Steak Cook-Off is held annually in Magnolia, Arkansas.

Barbeque Sauce

1 cup vinegar
⅔ cup lemon juice
2 teaspoons minced garlic
1 onion, finely grated
1 cup brown sugar
4 cups ketchup
1 tablespoon salt
1 teaspoon cayenne pepper
1 tablespoon black pepper
¼ cup prepared mustard
2 teaspoons liquid smoke

In saucepan over medium heat, combine vinegar, lemon juice, garlic, onion, and sugar and bring to boil. Add remaining ingredients to saucepan and boil for 5 minutes.

The international Bar-B-Q Festival in Owensboro, Kentucky awards the Governor's Cup for the best barbeque.

Almond Chicken

4 boneless, skinless chicken breast halves
Salt and pepper
3 tablespoons butter
1 (6 ounce) can frozen orange juice concentrate,
** thawed**
½ teaspoon salt
¼ teaspoon pepper
½ cup salted almonds, toasted
2 tablespoons bourbon
Hot, cooked rice

Season chicken with salt and pepper. In skillet, brown chicken in butter over medium heat and reduce heat to low. Add orange juice, ½ teaspoon salt and ¼ teaspoon pepper. Cover and cook over medium heat for 25 minutes. Spoon sauce over chicken twice while it cooks. Remove chicken to serving platter and keep warm.

Add bourbon to sauce in skillet, stir and heat. Pour mixture over chicken and serve over hot, cooked rice. Sprinkle with almonds.

Chicken Breasts Supreme

4 boneless, skinless chicken breast halves
¼ cup (½ stick) butter
½ teaspoon salt
⅛ teaspoon pepper
1 (10 ounce) can condensed cream of chicken soup
¾ cup sauterne or chicken broth
1 (8½ ounce) can water chestnuts, drained, sliced
1 (4 ounce) can sliced mushrooms, drained
2 tablespoons chopped green peppers
¼ teaspoon crushed thyme leaves

Preheat oven to 350°. In skillet, brown chicken in butter on all sides. Arrange chicken in ungreased 9 x 13-inch pan. Sprinkle with salt and pepper.

Add soup to butter in fry pan and slowly stir in sauterne or broth. Add remaining ingredients and heat to boil. Pour soup mixture over chicken. Cover and bake for 45 minutes. Remove cover and bake 15 minutes longer.

Chicken Divan

2 (10 ounce) packages frozen broccoli
4 boneless, skinless chicken breast halves, cooked,
  sliced
2 (10 ounce) cans cream of chicken soup
1 cup mayonnaise
1 teaspoon lemon juice
½ teaspoon curry powder or Worcestershire sauce
1½ cups shredded sharp cheese, divided
½ cup dry, seasoned breadcrumbs
1 teaspoon butter, melted

Preheat oven to 350°. In saucepan, cook broccoli until tender and
drain. Arrange broccoli in sprayed 9 x 13-inch baking dish. Place
chicken slices on top.

In bowl, combine soup, mayonnaise, lemon juice, curry or
Worcestershire sauce and ¾ cup cheese and pour over chicken.
In separate bowl, combine breadcrumbs and butter and layer over
chicken. Sprinkle remaining cheese over top and bake for
25 to 30 minutes.

*On August 5, 1864, at the Battle of Mobile Bay,
Admiral David Farragut issued his famous command,
"Damn the torpedoes, full speed ahead."*

Chicken Souffle Special

15 slices white bread
6 boneless, skinless chicken breast halves, cooked
½ cup mayonnaise
1 cup grated cheddar cheese, divided
5 large eggs
2 cups milk
1 teaspoon salt
1 (10 ounce) can cream of mushroom soup

Butter bread slices on 1 side and remove crusts. Butter 9 x 13-inch baking dish and line bottom with 8 bread slices. Cover with chicken slices, spread with mayonnaise and sprinkle with ½ cup cheese. (You could use deli–sliced chicken instead of cooking chicken breasts.) Top with remaining 8 slices bread. Beat eggs, milk and salt and pour over entire casserole. Chill overnight or all day.

Preheat oven to 350°. When ready to bake, spread soup over top and press down with back of spoon. Bake covered for 45 minutes. Uncover, sprinkle with remaining ½ cup cheddar cheese, return to oven and bake for 15 minutes longer.

Burial mounds found in Arkansas were a prominent feature of the region's last prehistoric culture called the Mississippian, which began about 7 AD.

Poppy Seed Chicken

6 boneless, skinless chicken breast halves
1 (10 ounce) can cream of chicken soup
1 (8 ounce) carton sour cream
½ cup dry white wine or cooking wine
1½ cups (1 stack) round buttery crackers
1 cup chopped almonds, toasted
½ cup (1 stick) butter, melted
2 to 3 tablespoons poppy seeds

Preheat oven to 350°. Place chicken breasts in sprayed
9 x 13-inch baking pan and set aside.

In saucepan, combine soup, sour cream and wine and heat just
until it mixes. Pour soup mixture over chicken. Combine cracker
crumbs, almonds and butter and sprinkle over casserole. Sprinkle
with poppy seeds and bake for 45 minutes. Serve over rice or
noodles.

Succulent Pecan-Chicken Breasts

⅓ cup (⅔ stick) butter
1 cup flour
1 cup finely ground pecans
¼ cup sesame seeds
1 tablespoon paprika
1 teaspoon salt
¼ teaspoon pepper
1 egg, beaten
1 cup buttermilk
6 to 8 boneless, skinless chicken breast halves
⅓ cup coarsely chopped pecans

Preheat oven to 350°. Melt butter in large 9 x 13-inch baking dish and set aside. Combine flour, pecans, sesame seeds, paprika, salt and pepper.

Combine egg and buttermilk in separate bowl. Dip chicken in egg mixture, dredge in flour mixture and coat well. Place chicken in baking dish and turn once to coat with butter. Sprinkle with chopped pecans and bake for 40 minutes or until golden brown. Garnish with fresh parsley or sage.

Tip: *Chicken may be cut into strips, prepared the same way and used as an appetizer. A honey-mustard dressing would be nice for dipping. This recipe could also be used for fish, like orange roughy if cooking time is reduced to half.*

Yummy Barbequed-Grilled Chicken

6 boneless, skinless chicken breast halves
3 cups ketchup
½ cup packed brown sugar
¼ cup Worcestershire sauce
2 tablespoons vinegar
2 teaspoons seasoned salt
1 teaspoon hot sauce
½ teaspoon cracked black pepper

Wash and dry chicken breasts with paper towels. In saucepan, combine ketchup, brown sugar, Worcestershire sauce, vinegar, seasoned salt, hot sauce and pepper and mix well. Bring to boil, reduce heat to low and cook for 15 minutes.

Fire up grill and smoke chicken over mesquite wood, if possible. Baste chicken frequently with barbeque sauce. Turn chicken periodically and cook chicken 8 to 10 minutes per side. Any leftover barbeque sauce keeps well in refrigerator.

One of the few remaining unpolluted, free-flowing rivers in the lower 48 states is the Buffalo River.

Tootsie's Chicken Spectacular

2 cups diced, cooked chicken
1 (15 ounce) can green beans, drained
1 cup cooked white rice
1 (10 ounce) can cream of celery, chicken or
  mushroom soup
½ cup mayonnaise
½ cup sliced water chestnuts
2 tablespoons chopped pimiento
2 tablespoons chopped onion
¼ teaspoon salt
Dash pepper

Preheat oven to 350°. In bowl, combine ingredients and mix well. Place in 1½-quart baking dish and bake for 25 to 30 minutes.

Tip: This is a great recipe for leftover turkey.

> *Mardi Gras was introduced to the western*
> *world by Alabama. It was a celebration held*
> *on Shrove Tuesday, the before Lent.*

Chicken Elegant
This is rich, but worth the calories!

3 tablespoons butter
3 tablespoons flour
1¾ cups milk
½ cup shredded sharp American cheese
½ cup shredded Swiss cheese
½ teaspoon Worcestershire sauce
1 cup diced, cooked chicken or turkey
1 cup diced, cooked ham
1 (3 ounce) can sliced mushrooms, drained
2 tablespoons chopped pimiento
Toast points or hot, cooked noodles

Melt butter in saucepan and blend in flour. Add milk all at once, cook and stir until sauce is thick and bubbly. Remove from heat, add cheeses and stir until they melt.

Stir in Worcestershire sauce, chicken or turkey, ham, mushrooms and pimiento. Heat thoroughly and serve over toast points or hot, cooked noodles.

The oldest state-funded archival agency in the nation is the Alabama Department of Archives.

Tasty Chicken Casserole

1 onion, chopped
1 cup sliced celery
3 tablespoons butter
4 cups diced, cooked chicken
1 (6 ounce) package long grain and wild rice with
seasoning packet, cooked
1 (10 ounce) can cream of celery soup
1 (10 ounce) can cream of chicken soup
1 (4 ounce) jar pimentos, drained
2 (15 ounce) cans French-style green beans, drained
1 cup slivered almonds
1 cup mayonnaise
½ teaspoon salt
1 teaspoon black pepper
2½ cups crushed potato chips

Preheat oven to 350°. In small saucepan, sauté onion and celery in butter and pour into larger saucepan with chicken, rice, soups, pimentos, green beans, almonds, mayonnaise, salt and pepper. Pour into sprayed 10 x 15-inch baking dish. (This recipe needs a very large baking dish.)

Sprinkle crushed potato chips over casserole and bake uncovered for 35 minutes or until potato chips are slightly brown.

Old-Fashioned Chicken Spaghetti

8 to 10 ounces spaghetti
1 bell pepper, chopped
1 onion, chopped
1 cup chopped celery
½ cup (1 stick) butter
1 (10 ounce) can tomato soup
1 (10 ounce) can diced tomatoes and green chilies
1 (4 ounce) can chopped mushrooms, drained
½ teaspoon salt
½ teaspoon pepper
½ teaspoon garlic powder
3 teaspoons dry chicken bouillon
½ cup water
4 to 5 cups chopped chicken or turkey
1 (8 ounce) package cubed, processed cheese
1 (8 ounce) package shredded cheddar cheese

Preheat oven to 325°. Cook spaghetti according to package directions and drain. In medium saucepan, sauté bell pepper, onion and celery in butter. Add soup, tomatoes, mushrooms, salt, pepper, garlic powder, bouillon and water and mix.

In large mixing bowl, combine spaghetti, vegetable-soup mixture, chicken and cheese. Place in 2 (2-quart) sprayed baking dishes. Freeze one and bake the other covered for 40 to 50 minutes. To cook frozen casserole, thaw first.

Tip: This is a good recipe for leftover turkey.

Southern Fried Chicken

1 whole chicken, cut up
Salt
Pepper
2 eggs, beaten
2 tablespoons cream
Flour
Oil or shortening

Wash chicken pieces and dry with paper towels. Sprinkle all sides
with salt and pepper. Combine eggs and cream. Dip chicken
into egg mixture, dredge in flour and coat well. Carefully place
chicken in heavy skillet with ¼-inch oil or shortening and cover.
Over medium heat, brown chicken on both sides. Lower heat and
cook 25 minutes or until tender.

Gravy:

3 tablespoons flour
½ teaspoon salt
½ teaspoon pepper
1½ cups whole milk

Remove chicken from skillet and add 3 tablespoons flour, salt and
pepper and stir constantly. Increase stove temperature to HIGH.
Add milk, cook and stir until gravy is thick. Serve hot.

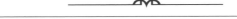

Miss Sadie: *"Honey, if you want to make someone*
happy just learn how to cook good fried chicken!"

Deep-Fried Chicken

1 whole chicken, cut up
Salt and pepper
1 cup flour
2 eggs
2 cups milk
1 teaspoon lemon juice

Wash and pat dry chicken with paper towels. Season chicken with salt and pepper. In bowl, combine flour, eggs, milk and lemon juice and mix thoroughly.

Dredge chicken in batter and fry in deep fryer over medium to high heat until golden brown.

Milk Gravy

3 to 4 tablespoons bacon drippings
⅓ cups flour
Salt and pepper
1½ cups milk

After frying bacon, pour drippings off and leave 3 to 4 tablespoons drippings. Add flour to skillet and add liberal amounts of salt and pepper.

Cook and stir until flour is light brown. Slowly add milk and stir constantly. Cool until mixture is thick.

Roasted Chicken Supreme

This is such an easy recipe and good for any meal.

1 (3 pound) whole chicken
1 whole onion
1 rib celery
Pure vegetable oil
Paprika

Preheat oven to 325°. Wash chicken and dry with paper towels. Cut celery in half. Insert onion and celery into chicken cavity. Tie legs, rub chicken with oil and sprinkle with paprika.

Roast in open pan for 35 minutes per pound of chicken. Baste every 40 minutes. To serve, remove onion and celery. (You can save and reuse for soup or stew.) Chicken will be extra juicy and moist with no onion flavor.

The Mount Pleasant community in South Carolina's Low Country has had sweet grass basket-making for more than 300 years. It is a traditional art form that has been passed for several generations.

Finger-Lickin' Smoked Chicken

3 whole chickens, cut in half
Seasoned pepper
½ cup (1 stick) butter
2 teaspoons Worcestershire sauce
2 dashes hot sauce
2 tablespoons lemon juice
½ teaspoon garlic salt
8 ounces 7-Up

Sprinkle chickens with seasoned pepper and leave at room temperature for 1 hour. In small saucepan, melt butter and add Worcestershire sauce, hot sauce, lemon juice and garlic salt and 7-Up.

Cook chickens on grill using mesquite charcoal. Turn often and baste with sauce mixture several times. Grill for about 1 hour and baste once more to keep chicken moist.

The Cumberland Gap National Historical Park is the largest national historical park in the U.S. With more than 20,000 acres of wilderness, 80% of the park has no paved roads. Majestic vistas may be seen from more than 55 miles of hiking trails and at the eastern end of the park it is possible to the Smoky Mountains more than 80 miles away.

Old-Fashioned Chicken and Dumplings

2 pounds boneless, skinless chicken breasts
½ onion, chopped
½ cup sliced celery
1 carrot, sliced
1 teaspoon salt
½ teaspoon black pepper
3 tablespoons shortening
2 cups flour
1 teaspoon salt
9 tablespoons ice water

In a large kettle or soup pot, place chicken breasts and cover with water. Add onion, celery, carrot, salt and pepper. Cover and cook for 40 minutes or until chicken is tender. Remove chicken and break into bite-size pieces. Strain broth and return to large pot.

In large bowl, cut shortening into flour and salt with pastry blender or fork until dough is pea-size. Add 1 tablespoon ice water at a time and mix lightly with fork. On floured surface, roll dough very thinly and keep roller well floured. Cut into strips and layer on wax paper. Chill for 45 minutes.

Bring broth and chicken pieces to a boil. Drop strips into boiling broth and chicken pieces. Do not stir but jiggle or shake pot. (Stirring will break up dumplings.) Cook on medium heat for 30 minutes.

Family-Secret Chicken and Noodles

This is a great recipe to prepare ahead of time and freeze.

¼ cup (½ stick) butter
½ cup flour
½ teaspoon each basil, parsley, salt
1 pint milk
1 (4 ounce) can sliced mushrooms, drained
1 (10 ounce) can cream of mushroom soup
1 (2 ounce) jar diced pimientos
1 (4 pound) stewing hen, cooked, diced
1 (14 ounce) can chicken broth
1 (16 ounce) package medium egg noodles
4 ounces grated cheddar or American cheese
Paprika

Preheat oven to 350°. In saucepan over medium heat, melt butter
and add flour and seasonings. Add milk slowly and stir constantly
until thick.

Add mushrooms, mushroom soup, pimientos, diced chicken and
chicken broth. Cook noodles according to package directions and
salt to taste. Drain.

Mix noodles with sauce and stir gently. Pour mixture into
9 x 13-inch baking dish. Sprinkle with cheese and paprika.
Cover and chill until baking time. Bake for 20 to 30 minutes
until it heats thoroughly.

Cranberry-Glazed Cornish Hens

6 Cornish hens
Salt and pepper
1 (16 ounce) can whole cranberry sauce
¼ cup (½ stick) butter
¼ cup frozen orange juice concentrate
2 teaspoons grated orange rind
Pinch of poultry seasoning
1 tablespoon brown sugar, optional

Preheat oven to 400°. Allow hens to thaw and wash them under cold water. Pat dry with paper towels and season inside and out. Place hens in shallow pan without rack and bake for 35 minutes.

In saucepan, heat cranberry sauce, butter, orange juice, orange rind and poultry seasoning. Pour mixture over hens. Lower oven temperature to 350° and continue to bake for an additional 30 minutes. Baste often with cranberry sauce until it browns well.

If desired, sprinkle brown sugar lightly over hens and slip under broiler to glaze.

Southern-Stuffed Peppers

6 large green peppers
½ pound chicken livers, chopped
6 slices bacon, diced
1 cup chopped onion
1 cup sliced celery
1 clove garlic, crushed
1 (4 ounce) can sliced mushrooms
2 cups cooked rice
1 teaspoon salt
¼ teaspoon pepper
Dash of cayenne pepper

Preheat oven to 375°. Wash peppers, cut slice from stem end and remove seeds. Cook peppers about 5 minutes in small amount of boiling, salt water. Remove from water and drain.

Cook chicken livers, bacon, onion, celery and garlic until vegetables are tender. Add mushrooms, rice and seasonings. Stuff peppers with mixture.

Arrange in baking pan, seal and freeze. To serve, thaw and add ½-inch water to pan, cover and bake for 20 to 25 minutes.

The Atlantic Flyway is a route for birds migrating along the Atlantic coast. It crosses Virginia, and the state provides important resting and feeding grounds.

Turkey Croquettes

*These are very easy to make. Make several
batches and freeze them for another meal.*

1½ cups cooked, chopped turkey
1 (10 ounce) can cream of chicken soup
1 cup turkey stuffing mix
2 eggs
1 tablespoon minced onion
Flour
Oil

Mix all ingredients in bowl and chill for several hours. Shape into
patties or rolls. Dredge in flour and fry in deep fat until brown.

*The first of the original 13 Colonies, Jamestown, was
founded for the purpose of silk cultivation to be traded
with the Court of King James. After fungus destroyed
the mulberry trees, tobacco was planted as a cash crop.*

Smoked Turkey

*This may sound incredible, but it works! The trick is teaching
your husband to smoke the turkey! Thanksgiving is much
more enjoyable with a "little help in the kitchen"!*

**1 butter-basted turkey
2 or 3 strips uncooked bacon
1 onion, peeled, halved
2 or 3 small ribs celery
Poultry seasoning, salt and pepper**

Soak hickory chips in water while charcoal gets "good and hot".
Buy turkey that will fit on covered grill. Place washed and dried
turkey in disposable aluminum foil roasting pan.

Insert onion and celery in cavity of turkey and rub poultry
seasoning, salt and pepper on turkey inside and out. Lay strips of
bacon across top of turkey.

Pour a little water in pan to prevent sticking and place on grill.
Close grill cover and cook for 11 minutes per pound. Baste
occasionally during cooking time. (This cooking method
produces a beautiful brown turkey. The meat will look slightly
pink due to the smoking procedure, but it is done!)

Pan drippings in roaster are ready to make gravy. By using this
procedure, Thanksgiving cooking is much easier because your
oven is free for other dishes. Just throw away the messy pan when
you are finished!

Carolina Country Ham

1 smoked ham
1 apple
1 onion
1 cup molasses
1 teaspoon mixed pickling spices
½ cup packed brown sugar
1 teaspoon Worcestershire sauce
1 (20 ounce) can pineapple slices, drained
Cloves

Soak ham overnight and clean thoroughly. Place ham in large container and cover with cold water. Add apple and onion. Pour in molasses and pickling spices. Simmer slowly for about 20 minutes per pound of ham.

Remove ham from heat just before meat falls off bone and cool in water. Skin, remove fat and place trimmed ham in baking dish.

Combine brown sugar and Worcestershire sauce. Cut pineapple into halves forming crescents. Spread brown sugar over ham and place pineapple halves in rows over brown sugar. Pierce each slice with cloves. Bake at 275° for 20 minutes or until sugar glaze is brown.

Miss Sadie: *"Some Southerners think country ham is just not complete without Red Eye Gravy. My daddy loved it. He used the drippin's from the salty ham, added a little black coffee and made a thin, but wonderful gravy."*

Georgia Ham

1 Georgia country ham (about 12 pounds)
1½ cups brown sugar
1 cup bourbon

Preheat oven to 200°. Soak ham overnight in cold water and scrub with stiff brush. Change water a few times to rid ham of excess salt.

In bowl, combine brown sugar and bourbon and press into fat of ham. Place in roasting pan, cover and bake for 8 hours. DO NOT OPEN OVEN.

The tradition of cured, smoked country ham began in Smithfield, Virginia in the mid 1700's. The back part of a pig's thigh was salted, seasoned, smoked and aged to create one of the real delicacies of the South. Today Virginia country hams are considered some of the best in the world, but if you ask someone from Tennessee, Kentucky, North Carolina or Georgia, you will surely get an argument. Hams are usually slow-smoked with hickory, apple or pecan wood, salted, seasoned with blacked pepper and cured for 10 to 12 months.

Old-Fashioned Country Ham

Country ham, any size
1 cup brown sugar
2 tablespoons hot mustard
Coca cola
Whole cloves

Prepare recipe 1 day ahead. Soak ham in water overnight and wash with stiff brush. Place in roasting pan with 5 cups boiling water. Cover and place in cold oven. Turn on oven to 500° for 15 minutes and then turn oven off. Leave ham in oven for 3 hours and DO NOT OPEN DOOR. Turn oven to 500° again and cook for 15 minutes and then turn off. Leave ham in oven overnight and do not disturb.

Next day, cut off fat and score ham in diamond pattern. Combine brown sugar, hot mustard and enough cola to make a paste. Spread over ham and place whole cloves in each diamond. Bake in 350° oven for 30 minutes.

Virginia or Smithfield hams are the most famous country-cured hams in the U.S. and can only be cured and sold from the Smithfield, Virginia area.

Saucy Ham Loaf

Make this mustard sauce the day before you make the ham loaf.

Sweet-and-Hot Mustard Sauce:

4 ounces dry mustard
1 cup vinegar
3 eggs, beaten
1 cup sugar

Combine mustard and vinegar and mix until smooth. Set aside overnight. Cook eggs and sugar in double boiler and stir constantly for 8 to 10 minutes or until mixture coats spoon. Cool and refrigerate in covered jars.

Ham Loaf:

1 pound ground ham
½ pound ground beef
½ pound ground pork
2 eggs
1 cup bread or cracker crumbs
2 teaspoons Worcestershire sauce
1 (5 ounce) can evaporated milk
3 tablespoons chili sauce
1 teaspoon seasoned salt
1 teaspoon seasoned pepper
Bacon to strip top of loaf, optional

Ask butcher to grind 3 meats together for the ham loaf.

Preheat oven to 350°. In bowl, combine all loaf ingredients except bacon. Form into loaf in 9 x 13-inch baking pan. Strip bacon on top and bake for 1 hour.

Raisin Sauce for Ham

1 cup raisins
1 cup water
¼ cup vinegar
¼ cup packed brown sugar
1 teaspoon prepared mustard
1 teaspoon Worcestershire sauce
½ teaspoon salt
1 tablespoon flour
1 tablespoon butter

In saucepan, cook raisins in water for 10 minutes over medium heat. Remove from heat and set aside.

In bowl, combine remaining ingredients and add to tender raisins. Cook mixture until thick and add butter, if desired.

The Virginia variety of peanut is the one used for roasting because it has the largest kernels. This variety is grown mostly in southeastern Virginia and northeastern North Carolina.

Pork Chops and Red Cabbage

6 (1-inch thick) pork chops
⅓ cup flour
⅓ cup sugar
½ cup cider vinegar
¼ cup water
1 small red cabbage, shredded
2 Rome apples, with peel, sliced

In large skillet with a little oil, brown pork chops on both sides. Lower heat, cover and simmer for 15 minutes.

In small bowl, combine flour, sugar, and liberal amount of salt. Combine vinegar and water separately.

In larger bowl, combine cabbage and apples and toss with flour-sugar mixture and then vinegar mixture. Spoon over pork chops, cover and simmer for 30 minutes.

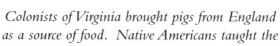

Colonists of Virginia brought pigs from England as a source of food. Native Americans taught the colonists their methods for curing venison and they adapted the salting, smoking and aging to hams.

Pan-Fried Pork Chops

Look for Miss Sadies' comment for another
step to these wonderful pork chops.

Salt and pepper
6 to 8 thin pork chops
¾ cup flour
¼ cup extra virgin olive oil

Salt and pepper pork chops and dredge in flour. Pat flour into
pork chops so it will stick.

Carefully place pork chops into skillet with hot oil and brown on
both sides. Make sure center cooks well.

---

*Miss Sadie: "I always pan-fried my pork chops and I
always had people coming back. One day after I browned
those pork chops, I added a little water to my lovely
cast-iron skillet and baked them in the oven. It
was 350° for about 45 minutes and those
pork chops just fell apart."*

Pork Chop Casserole

¾ cup uncooked rice
6 pork chops, floured
1 large onion, chopped
1 medium bell pepper, cut in rings
2 tablespoons cooking oil
1 (15 ounce) can diced tomatoes
¼ teaspoon thyme
¼ teaspoon marjoram
1 teaspoon salt
1 (10 ounce) can beef broth

Preheat oven to 350°. Place rice in 2-quart shallow baking dish. Brown floured chops in oil and place on top of rice.

Brown onion and bell pepper in remaining oil and pour over pork chops. Combine tomatoes, thyme, marjoram and salt and pour over pork chops. Pour beef broth over entire casserole. Cover and bake for 1 hour.

Chitlins is the informal name given to the intestines of animals that are cooked for human consumption. They originated with the African-American slaves who were given the leftovers from cured hams.

Barbequed Pork Chops

6 pork chops
1 tablespoon chili powder
1 teaspoon salt
1 teaspoon paprika
¼ cup packed brown sugar
½ cup vinegar
1 (10 ounce) can tomato soup

Preheat oven to 350°. Place pork chops in baking dish.

In bowl, combine remaining ingredients and pour over chops.
Bake for 1 hour, 30 minutes.

Miss Sadie: *"Southerners know how to cook barbeque
and don't you let anyone tell you different."*

Pork Loin with Apricot Glaze

1 (3½ to 4 pound) center-cut pork loin
1 tablespoon olive oil
Seasoned pepper
1 teaspoon dried rosemary
1 cup dry white wine or cooking wine
1 cup water
1½ cups apricot preserves

Preheat oven to 350°. Rub loin with olive oil and sprinkle seasoned pepper and rosemary over top. Place in shallow roasting pan, pour wine and water over loin and cook loin for 1 hour.

Remove from oven and spoon 1 cup pan drippings into small bowl. Add apricot preserves to drippings and mix well. Pour apricot mixture over pork in pan, turn oven temperature down to 325° and return to oven. Continue to cook for 1 additional hour and baste 2 to 3 times with pan drippings. Remove from oven and set aside to cool for 15 minutes before slicing.

To cook day before, cook as directed and let roast cool. Take roast out of drippings, place in glass baking dish and slice. Place drippings in separate container and chill both. When ready to serve, heat drippings and pour over roast. Warm in oven at 350° for 20 minutes.

Grilled Pork Loin

½ teaspoon garlic powder
¼ teaspoon celery salt
½ teaspoon onion salt
2 tablespoons lemon juice
1 (5 pound) pork loin

In bowl, combine garlic powder, salts and lemon juice. Rub mixture into tenderloin and place in covered glass dish. Chill for at least 8 hours or overnight.

Grill tenderloin over hot coals for 30 minutes or until thickest portion of meat reaches 140°. (Center part of tenderloin will be slightly pink.) Set aside for at least 10 minutes before cutting.

The annual Pig Cookin' Contest is the largest whole hog cooking contest in the U.S. It is held in April in Newport, North Carolina.

Carolina Pulled Pork

Lots of people in the South eat their coleslaw
right on the bun with the pork. It's great!

3 onions, sliced, divided
1 (3 to 4 pound) pork roast or shoulder
Carolina-style barbeque sauce with mustard
Buns
Dill pickles

Place onion rings from 1 onion in bottom of slow cooker and
place roast on top. Add remaining sliced onions over top of roast
and fill slow cooker about half way or a little more with water.
Cook over low heat overnight.

Remove roast and pour out all but 1 to 2 inches of water from
slow cooker. When roast is cool, pull meat apart with fingers
or shred it with fork. Return roast to slow cooker and pour
barbeque sauce over meat.

Chop remaining onion, season with salt and pepper and add to
meat. Cook on high for several hours until onion is tender. Serve
on large buns with coleslaw, dill pickles and sliced onions.

Tip: If your barbeque sauce is thick, you may need a little more stock
from slow cooker so meat will not be dry.

Barbequed Pork Roast

5 pound pork roast, boned, trimmed
2 onions, sliced
6 cloves
2 cups water
1 large onion, chopped
1 (16 ounce) bottle barbeque sauce

Place half onion slices in slow cooker. Add meat, cloves and water and top with remaining sliced onions. Cover and cook overnight or 8 to 12 hours on LOW.

Discard drippings. Remove and shred meat. Return to slow cooker along with chopped onions and barbeque sauce. Cook on HIGH for 2 hours and stir occasionally. Serve roast on buns.

Lexington, North Carolina considers itself the Barbeque Capital of the World. Its annual Barbeque Festival is held in October.

Ginger Baby-Back Ribs

1 tablespoon butter
1 onion, chopped
1 cup apricot preserves
¼ cup soy sauce
4 tablespoons honey
3 tablespoons red wine
1 tablespoon fresh grated ginger
1 tablespoon dried orange peel
4 to 5 pounds baby-back pork ribs

Preheat oven to 375°. Melt butter in saucepan and cook onion until tender, but not brown. Add apricot preserves, soy sauce, honey, wine, ginger and orange peel. Cook and stir constantly until mixture heats thoroughly.

Place ribs in large baking pan and pour preserve mixture over ribs. Cover and bake for 30 minutes. Reduce heat to 275° and bake 3 hours to 3 hours, 30 minutes or until rib meat is tender. (If ribs have not browned, remove cover and bake another 15 minutes.)

The World Championship Barbeque Cooking Contest is held annually in Memphis, Tennessee in May. It is billed as the largest pork barbeque cooking contest on the planet.

Low Country Boil

3 pounds kielbasa or link sausage
4 potatoes with peels
3 onions
3 cups cut green beans, drained
Water to cover

Cut sausage into bite-size pieces. Wash potatoes and peel onions.
Place sausage, potatoes, whole onions and green beans into large
stockpot, cover with water and boil until potatoes are tender.
Season mixture according to your own taste.

Savory Sausage and Sweet Potatoes

1 pound sausage
2 large sweet potatoes, peeled, sliced
3 Granny smith apples, peeled, sliced
⅓ cup sugar
1 tablespoon flour

Preheat oven to 350°. Form sausage into small balls and fry
in skillet until well done. Drain sausage. In buttered 2-quart
casserole dish, arrange potatoes, apples and sausage balls in layers.

In bowl, combine sugar, flour and ½ cup water and mix well.
Pour mixture over layers and cover. Bake for 40 minutes or until
potatoes are tender.

Sausage Souffle

8 slices white bread, cubed
2 cups shredded sharp cheddar cheese
1½ pounds link sausage cut in thirds
4 eggs
2¼ cups milk
¾ teaspoon dry mustard
1 (10 ounce) can cream of mushroom soup
½ cup milk

Grease 9 x 13-inch baking dish with butter. Place bread cubes in dish and top with cheese.

Brown and drain sausage and place on top of cheese. Beat eggs with milk and mustard and pour over sausage. Cover and chill overnight.

Preheat oven to 300°. Dilute soup with ½ cup milk and pour over bread and sausage. Bake 1 hour or until set.

Sweet potatoes are high in vitamins C, E and beta-carotene, a form of vitamin A. Beta-carotene is the source of yellow, red and orange pigments in fruits and vegetables. It is an extremely important nutrient needed to maintain good health and to reduce the risk of diseases.

Supreme Ham Casserole

2 cups cubed, cooked ham or left-over ham
1 onion, chopped
1 sweet red bell pepper, chopped
2 ribs celery, chopped
1 (6 ounce) box white and wild rice, uncooked
1 (4 ounce) jar pimento, drained
1 (8 ounce) package shredded Colby cheese
2 (10 ounce) cans cream of chicken soup

Preheat oven to 350°. In large bowl, combine all ingredients plus amount of water called for on box of rice. Mix well.

Spoon mixture into sprayed 9 x 13-inch baking dish. Cover and bake for 1 hour.

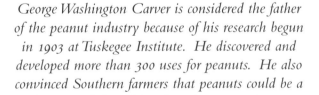

George Washington Carver is considered the father of the peanut industry because of his research begun in 1903 at Tuskegee Institute. He discovered and developed more than 300 uses for peanuts. He also convinced Southern farmers that peanuts could be a cash crop and should be planted as a rotation crop. Agriculture in the South was changed forever.

Great Sandwich Loaf

1 loaf unsliced French bread
½ cup mayonnaise
⅓ cup fresh, chopped parsley
2 (8 ounce) packages cream cheese, softened
1 cup shredded Swiss cheese
½ cup finely chopped onion
¼ teaspoon salt
1 teaspoon lemon juice
1 tablespoon Worcestershire sauce
8 slices boiled ham
Dill pickles, sliced lengthwise

Slice bread in half. Hollow out each half with fork and leave
½-inch thick shell (save inside for crumbs). Spread mayonnaise
in hollow and sprinkle parsley. In bowl, combine cream cheese,
Swiss cheese, onion, salt, lemon and Worcestershire sauce and
blend until creamy.

Spoon mixture into bread halves and pack down. Leave ridge in
center. Roll pickles in ham slices and place rolls end to end down
center of loaf.

Place bread halves together, wrap in foil and chill. To serve, cut
loaf into 1-inch slices.

Baked Rockfish Flounder

2 to 3 pounds fish, whole flounder
3 or more strips bacon
4 medium-sized potatoes
2 or more onions
1 (8 ounce) can tomato sauce
Pepper
1 lemon cut in wedges
Parsley

Preheat oven to 325°. Salt fish inside and out and cut slits on top. Place in sprayed glass baking dish. With knife blade, press strips of bacon into slits. Bake in hot oven until fish browns. Remove from oven.

Steam potatoes and onion until tender and arrange ring of potatoes and onion over baked fish. Pour tomato sauce and enough water over fish to keep it moist. (Use water from onions and potatoes. Make sure water is still warm. Never add cold water to anything you cook). Add pepper as desired.

Return dish to oven and cook for 20 minutes or until done. Baste once. Garnish dish with lemon wedges and parsley before serving.

The Eastern Shore Seafood Festival in Chincoteague, Virginia is held in May. It is an "All You Can Eat" festival and features Little Neck, Steamed Clams, Oysters On The Half Shell, Fried Clams and Fried Fish, Chicken Tenders and Chowder, French-Fried Sweet Potatoes, Cole Slaw and Hush Puppies.

Seaside Red Snapper

1 (3 to 5 pound) whole, butterflied red snapper
½ cup (1 stick) butter, melted
Flour
Cracked black pepper
Sea salt
Fresh dill weed
White wine
1 cucumber, sliced
Paprika

Preheat oven to 350°. Rinse and pat dry inside and outside of red snapper. Brush melted butter on inside and outside of snapper, but reserve some for later. Sprinkle flour, salt and pepper on inside and outside of snapper thoroughly. Place fresh dill weed inside fish and close.

Spray or butter inside of baking dish and pour 3 to 4 tablespoons white wine on bottom of dish. Carefully lay snapper in dish and bake for 20 minutes. Remove dish from oven, baste with reserved melted butter and add a little white wine if needed.

Return to oven and bake additional 20 to 25 minutes or until fish flakes. Remove dill weed. Carefully place whole snapper on serving plate and garnish with cucumber slices and dashes of paprika.

Low Country Muddle

"Muddle" is a term used by early settlers meaning "a mess of fish".
It's a basic measurement that all Southerners understand.

2 large bell peppers, cored, chopped
4 ribs celery, chopped
2 onions, chopped
2 cloves garlic, minced
Oil
6 cups clam juice
10 to 12 clams, cleaned
10 to 12 mussels, cleaned
10 to 12 shrimp
1 to 1½ pounds flounder

In large stockpot, cook bell pepper, celery, onions and garlic in a little oil until onions are translucent. Pour in clam juice and clams. Cook until clams open. Add mussels, shrimp and flounder. Cook until shrimp turns pink.

Tip: Throw away any clams or mussels that didn't open.

The Annual World Catfish Festival is held in Belzoni, Mississippi. Belzoni is the Catfish Capital of the World.

Fried Catfish

The best frying is done in an iron skillet and everybody in the South knows that. So the best thing you can do with this recipe is to start with an iron skillet.

Fresh catfish filets
Cracker crumbs or cornmeal
Canola oil

Wash and pat dry filets. Pour cracker crumbs or cornmeal in shallow bowl and add a little salt and pepper. Dredge filets in crumbs and coat well.

Pour enough oil in skillet to cover fish about halfway. When oil is very hot, carefully add filets one at a time and place them in skillet. When fish is crispy and golden brown on 1 side, turn and cook until crispy and golden brown on other side. Serve hot.

The Catfish Capital of the World is considered to be Belzoni, Mississippi.

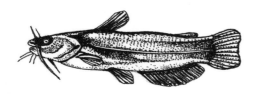

Crisp Oven-Fried Fish

¼ cup milk
1 egg, beaten
1 cup corn flake crumbs
¼ teaspoon thyme
¼ cup parmesan cheese
2 pounds fish filets
⅓ cup (⅔ stick) butter, melted
Parsley
Lemon

Preheat oven to 425°. Combine milk and egg and pour into shallow pan. Mix flake crumbs, thyme and cheese in separate shallow pan.

Dip filet in milk-egg mixture, roll in crumb-cheese mixture and place side-by-side in sprayed baking dish. Drizzle with melted butter.

Pour remaining crumbs over top and bake for 12 to 15 minutes. Serve with parsley and lemon.

Shrimp-Asparagus Casserole

¼ cup (½ stick) butter
24 saltines, coarsely rolled
2 (16 ounce) cans green asparagus spears
4 eggs, hard-boiled, sliced
1½ pounds shrimp, boiled, chopped coarsely
1 (10 ounce) can cream of mushroom soup
¾ cup milk
1 tablespoon onion juice
1 (8 ounce) package shredded cheddar cheese

Preheat oven to 325°. Grease 8 x 12-inch baking dish with butter and place half cracker crumbs on bottom. Layer asparagus, eggs and shrimp. Lightly salt and pepper each layer as you build casserole.

Combine soup, milk and onion juice and pour over casserole mixture. Sprinkle top with cheese and remaining crumbs, dot with remaining butter and bake for 20 minutes.

The Old Spanish Fort Museum in Pascagoula, Mississippi has the world's largest shrimp on display.

Shrimp Mousse

Easy! Prepare day ahead and store in refrigerator.
Use as appetizer, salad or main dish.

1 (10 ounce) can condensed tomato soup
1½ tablespoons unflavored gelatin
½ cup cold water
2 (3 ounce) packages cream cheese, softened
1 cup mayonnaise
1 tablespoon prepared horseradish
1 tablespoon Worcestershire sauce
½ teaspoon salt
2 cups cooked, finely chopped shrimp
1 cup celery, finely chopped
⅓ fresh or frozen onions, chopped

Heat soup to boil. In large bowl, soften gelatin in cold water. Pour hot soup over gelatin and stir until it dissolves. Beat in cream cheese and next four ingredients. Stir in shrimp, celery, and onions and pour mixture into 1½-quart mold. Chill until firm overnight or 24 hours. Unmold on platter.

Tip: Mold into square-shaped baking dish and cut out in separate
servings for luncheon or dinner entree. Serve on lettuce leaf with
green vegetable and lemon tart.

Low Country Shrimp Boil

2 pounds kielbasa or link sausage
8 large ears corn-on-the cob, halved
14 to 16 new potatoes with peels
2 onions
1 to 2 tablespoons salt
Shrimp boil or Old Bay crab boil
Water
4 to 5 pounds shrimp in shells

In large stockpot, place sausage, cut in bite-size pieces, corn-on-the-cob, new potatoes, onions, seasoning and enough water to cover. Bring to boil and cook for 15 to 20 minutes or until potatoes are almost tender.

Add shrimp and cook for another 5 minutes or until shrimp turn pink. Drain and serve.

The low country of South Carolina is the coastal plain of the state. First settled more than 300 years ago by English settlers and slaves from Barbados, the area is rich in history and local traditions. Rice brought great wealth to planters and hard work for the African-Americans who supplied the labor.

Many of the traditional dishes from the region include rice, shrimp, crab oysters, fried okra and fried chicken, just to name a few.

Fried Shrimp

Have a little patience with these and you'll be well rewarded.

Fresh shrimp
Lemons
Cayenne pepper, optional
Flour
Salt and pepper
Eggs
Cracker crumbs or cornmeal
Canola oil

Wash shrimp, remove veins and shells (except for last segment), but keep tails. Spread tails and press down with large spoon. Squeeze fresh lemon juice generously over shrimp. Sprinkle cayenne pepper lightly over shrimp and marinate shrimp in refrigerator for 30 minutes.

Mix flour with salt and pepper in shallow bowl. Dredge shrimp through flour and coat generously. Set aside for 30 minutes.

Dip shrimp in beaten egg and dredge in cracker crumbs. Deep-fry shrimp in very hot oil and carefully add shrimp one at a time to cook. When shrimp is crispy and golden brown, remove from oil and drain well.

The unusual ecosystem of South Carolina's low country provides habitat for alligator, blue heron, egret, anhinga, bald eagle and migratory waterfowl.

Favorite Salmon Croquettes

What shape were your croquettes? Were they round
logs, flat patties or triangular-shaped logs? No
matter how you shape them, these are great!

1 (15 ounce) can salmon
½ teaspoon seasoned salt
½ teaspoon black pepper
¼ cup shrimp cocktail sauce or chili sauce
1 (10 ounce) can cream of chicken soup, divided
1 egg
½ onion, finely chopped
Several dashes hot sauce
1⅓ cups cracker crumbs
Flour
Oil

Drain salmon well in colander and remove skin and little back
bones. In mixing bowl, combine salmon, seasoned salt, pepper,
cocktail sauce, ½-can soup, egg, onion, hot sauce and cracker
crumbs and mix well.

Pat mixture into logs with 3 sides about 3 inches long and roll in
flour. Make about 10 to 12 logs. Pour just enough oil in large
skillet to cover bottom. Turn to medium heat, place croquettes in
skillet and fry. Turn twice so you have 3 sides that brown. (Add
extra tablespoon oil halfway through cooking if needed.)

It will take about 15 minutes to fry on 3 sides. (Of course you
could deep-fry croquettes if you want.) Use remaining cream of
chicken soup by diluting with equal parts of milk and have a cup
of soup as an appetizer.

Salmon Patties

1 (16 ounce) can salmon, flaked
¼ teaspoon pepper
1 tablespoon prepared mustard
2 eggs, beaten
½ cup milk
1 tablespoon flour
Soda cracker crumbs (about 4 crackers)
Corn oil
Lemon wedges

In bowl, combine salmon, pepper and mustard and mix well. In heavy pan, mix eggs, milk and flour and cook slowly. Stir constantly until thick. Add salmon mixture and cracker crumbs. Cool and form into patties.

Heat corn oil in skillet and fry patties on both sides until brown. Serve with lemon wedges.

The annual "Low Country Shrimp Festival
and Blessing of the Fleet" is held in May
in McClellanville, South Carolina.

Salmon Mousse

Do early in the day and store in refrigerator.

1 (1 ounce) package unflavored gelatin
¼ cup cold water
½ cup mayonnaise
1 tablespoon lemon juice
1 tablespoon onion, grated
½ teaspoon hot sauce
¼ teaspoon paprika
1 teaspoon salt
1 (15 ounce) can salmon, drained
1 tablespoon chopped capers
½ cup heavy cream
3 cups cottage cheese, drained

Soften gelatin in cold water, add boiling water and stir until it dissolves. Cool.

Add mayonnaise, lemon juice and onion and mix well. Blend in paprika, hot sauce and salt. Chill mixture until it reaches consistency of unbeaten egg white.

Add salmon and capers and beat well. Whip cream and fold into salmon mixture. Turn into 2-quart oiled mold. Cover top with cottage cheese. Chill for 2 hours until firm.

To serve, unmold on serving plate and garnish with watercress or lemon slices.

Savannah-Style Deviled Crabs

*Delicious for brunch, lunch or supper - - make in
advance and refrigerate until baking time.*

½ pound crabmeat
1 hard-boiled egg, diced
½ cup cracker crumbs
1½ tablespoons (¼ stick) butter, melted
1 tablespoon Worcestershire sauce
2 tablespoons dry sherry OR any dry white wine
¼ teaspoon hot sauce
¼ teaspoon salt
¼ cup plus 1 tablespoon mayonnaise
1 tablespoon dijon mustard
¼ teaspoon paprika
¼ teaspoon nutmeg
4 clean crab shells

Preheat oven to 350°. Carefully pick over crabmeat for bits of
shell. Toss crumbs in butter. Add remaining ingredients except
1 tablespoon mayonnaise and paprika. Mix well and pile into crab
shells.

"Ice" top of each mound with remaining mayonnaise and dust
with paprika. Bake for 15 minutes and place under broiler for
1 to 2 minutes or until mayonnaise topping puffs and browns
slightly.

Seacoast Crab Devils

2 tablespoons (¼ stick) butter
3 tablespoons flour
1 cup chicken broth
⅓ cup whipping cream
½ teaspoon salt
⅛ teaspoon cayenne pepper
2 egg yolks
1 (4 ounce) can sliced mushrooms
1 tablespoon dried parsley
2 (6 ounce) cans crabmeat, well-drained, flaked
6 ramekin shells
⅓ cup dry, seasoned breadcrumbs

Preheat oven to 350°. Melt butter in skillet over medium heat. Slowly mix in flour, broth and cream and stir well. Add salt, cayenne pepper and egg yolks and continue to stir and cook until thick. Add mushrooms, parsley and crabmeat to mixture and blend well.

Pour into lightly buttered shells or ramekins. Cover with breadcrumbs and bake for 10 minutes or until light brown.

The annual Savannah Seafood Festival is held in May in Savannah, Georgia.

Crab Delight

2 tablespoons chopped green pepper
2 tablespoons (¼ stick) butter
2 tablespoons flour
Dash cayenne pepper
½ teaspoon prepared mustard
¼ teaspoon salt
½ teaspoon Worcestershire sauce
1 cup chopped tomatoes, drained
1 cup shredded cheddar cheese
1 egg, slightly beaten
1⅔ cup scalded milk
1 cup flaked crabmeat
6 patty shells or toasted rounds

In saucepan, brown green pepper in butter and add flour and mix until smooth. In bowl, combine seasoning, tomatoes, cheese and egg and add to green pepper mixture.

Cook mixture in double boiler for 10 minutes. Stir constantly and add milk slowly. Add crabmeat and heat thoroughly. Serve on patty shells or toast rounds.

Betty Jo's Crab Cakes

1 pound crabmeat
1 large egg, lightly beaten
2 tablespoons minced onion
2 tablespoons mayonnaise
1 tablespoon Worcestershire sauce
1 tablespoon prepared mustard
½ to ¾ teaspoons hot sauce
1 teaspoon salt
½ teaspoon freshly ground pepper
¾ cup buttery cracker crumbs

In large bowl, combine all ingredients except cracker crumbs and mix well. Place cracker crumbs in shallow bowl. Shape crab mixture into 6 patties and roll in cracker crumbs.

In skillet, fry for about 3 minutes on each side. Drain.

Miss Sadie: *"Now, the best crab cakes I ever had were in Maryland. They were just some kind o' good."*

Mary Beth's Crab Casserole

1 pound fresh mushrooms
2 pounds crabmeat
2 cups mayonnaise
1 pint whipping cream
2 tablespoons chopped onion
2 tablespoons parsley
4 hard-boiled eggs, diced
1 (8 ounce) package herb stuffing mix

Preheat oven to 350°. Slice and sauté mushrooms. Mix all ingredients but save a little stuffing to be used for topping. Bake for 40 minutes in sprayed 9 x 13-inch pan.

Aunt Edna's Crabmeat Casserole

This is just as easy as can be.

½ cup chopped celery
½ cup chopped green pepper
¼ cup chopped onion
1 pound crabmeat
3 or 4 eggs, hard-boiled, chopped
1½ cups dry, seasoned breadcrumbs
1 cup mayonnaise
1 tablespoon dry mustard
1 tablespoon vinegar
1 tablespoon lemon juice
1 tablespoon dry horseradish
½ cup white wine
½ cup buttered breadcrumbs
Paprika

Preheat oven to 350°. Butter 1½-quart baking dish. Sauté celery, green pepper and onion until tender but not brown.

Combine all ingredients in prepared baking dish and top with buttered breadcrumbs. Sprinkle with paprika and bake for 20 minutes or until it heats thoroughly.

Elegant Luncheon Crab Quiche
Easy!

1 cup grated Swiss cheese
1 (6 ounce) can crabmeat
5 eggs
1½ cups milk or half-and-half cream
½ teaspoon salt
⅛ teaspoon black pepper
½ cup mushrooms, sliced
1 (9-inch) unbaked pie shell

Preheat oven to 375°. Sprinkle cheese into pie shell. Beat eggs and mix with milk and seasoning. Pour over cheese in pie shell and sprinkle with crabmeat. Bake for 35 to 55 minutes until firm.

Miss Sadie: *"I just love ladies' luncheon's especially now that hats are back."*

King Crab Casserole

**1 (10 ounce) package frozen broccoli spears or
  asparagus**
½ cup grated sharp cheddar cheese
6 tablespoons (¾ stick) butter, divided
2 tablespoons minced onion
2 tablespoons flour
¼ teaspoon curry powder
½ teaspoon salt
1 cup milk
1 tablespoon lemon juice
1 (6 ounce) package frozen king crab, thawed, drained
2 slices bread

Preheat oven to 350°. Cook broccoli or asparagus according
to package directions and drain. Arrange in sprayed 8 x 8-inch
baking dish, and sprinkle cheese over top.

Melt ¼ cup (½ stick) butter in saucepan, add onions and sauté
until soft. Add flour, seasonings and milk and stir constantly until
thick. Stir in lemon juice and add crab. Pour heated mixture over
broccoli or asparagus

Spread 2 tablespoons (¼ stick) butter over soft bread and cut into
cubes. Sprinkle over crab mixture and bake for 30 minutes.

Hard-Shell Blue Crabs

Blue crabs are the most popular Atlantic crab.

2 quarts water
8 to 10 live hard-shell blue crabs
Butter or cocktail sauce

Boil water in large slow cooker and drop several crabs in pot. Cover, boil several minutes and cook over low heat for 10 minutes. Remove with tongs and drain.

Remove tail flap on underneath side of crab. Remove hard shell on top. Remove legs and white gills on both sides of body. Discard all shells, gills and internal organs.

Use nutcracker to remove meat from legs and claws. Use small cocktail fork to remove meat from body. Break body in 2 pieces to reach all meat inside cavities.

Scalloped Oysters

½ cup (1 stick) butter
1 cup cracker crumbs
½ cup dry, seasoned breadcrumbs
1 pint oysters
Salt and pepper
2 tablespoons oyster liquid, divided
2 tablespoons light cream, divided

Preheat oven to 400°. Melt butter and pour into small bowl with cracker crumbs and breadcrumbs. Toss mixture to coat well.

Place ⅓ crumb mixture in shallow, sprayed baking dish and cover with half oysters. Sprinkle with salt and pepper according to your taste. Add to mixture 1 tablespoon of oyster liquid and 1 tablespoon light cream. Repeat process for second layer, top with remaining crumb mixture and bake for 30 minutes.

Miss Sadie: *"Honey, now don't you forget to say thank you, no sir and yes sir. It shows respect and you need to be respectful of your fellow man.*

Fried Oysters

Measurements just don't work with this recipe, so
just make sure you have enough of everything.

Fresh oysters, shucked
Cracker crumbs or cornmeal
Salt
Pepper
Canola oil

Wash and pat dry oysters. Pour cracker crumbs or cornmeal in shallow bowl and add a little salt and pepper. Roll oysters in crumbs and coat well.

Heat oil in deep fryer. When oil is very hot, carefully add oysters one at a time and place them so they do not touch. When oysters are crispy and golden brown, remove from oil and drain. Serve hot.

Tartar Sauce

⅓ cup drained sweet pickle relish
2 tablespoons minced onion
1½ cups mayonnaise

In bowl, combine all ingredients and mix well.

Smothered Quail, Southern Style

Salt and pepper
6 to 8 cleaned quail
Flour
½ cup (1 stick) butter
1½ cups milk

Salt and pepper quail and roll in flour. Melt butter in very large skillet, cover and brown quail over medium heat. Turn quail over several times. Remove quail and set aside.

Add 3 tablespoons flour and a little more salt and pepper to skillet and lightly brown flour. Slowly stir and cook in enough milk to make white gravy.

Return quail to skillet, roll in gravy and cover. Simmer over low heat for 45 minutes and baste every 15 minutes. Serve gravy over rice or biscuits.

Georgia is often recognized as the "Quail Capital of the World" and brings hunters from around the world. Two-thirds of the quail population can be lost with no reduction in the spring breeding population.

Billy Earl's Stewed Goose or Duck

Billy Earl's goose is stewed.

1 goose, cleaned, cut-up, parboiled
2 quarts water
2 tablespoons vegetable oil
Salt and pepper to taste
Flour dumplings (recipe below)

Place prepared fowl in large, heavy pot, cover with water and oil and bring to boil. Reduce heat and simmer 2 hours or until tender.

Turn heat up, bring to boil again and place dumplings in pot. Boil about 10 minutes. Reduce heat and simmer 1 hour and stir occasionally to prevent burning.

Flour Dumplings:

1 cup sifted flour
2 teaspoons baking powder
½ teaspoon salt
½ cup milk
2 tablespoons salad oil

Sift dry ingredients. Combine milk and oil and add to dry ingredients. Stir until mixture is just moist. Batter will be lumpy.

Drop by tablespoonfuls on top of bubbling stew. Cover tightly and bring to boil. Reduce heat and simmer 12 to 15 minutes without lifting cover of pot!

Barbequed Duck Breasts

1 (10 ounce) can cream of onion soup
½ cup ketchup
¼ cup (½ stick) butter
4 drops hot sauce
2 cloves garlic, finely chopped
¼ teaspoon salt
¼ teaspoon black pepper
2 ribs celery, sliced
1 green pepper, finely chopped
½ cup water
4 wild duck breasts
8 slices bacon

In saucepan, combine soup, ketchup, butter, hot sauce, garlic, salt, pepper, celery, bell pepper and water. Bring mixture to boil, reduce heat and simmer for 30 minutes. Cool. Remove each breast half from duck as intact as possible and remove skin.

To prepare duck, wrap each breast side with slice of bacon and secure with toothpick. Cover breasts with sauce and marinate for 3 hours in refrigerator. Grill over hot coals for 3 to 4 minutes on each side. Reheat remaining marinade for gravy.

Waterfowl along the Mississippi Flyway, whitetail deer, wild turkey and small game are plentiful in Arkansas.

Pine Bluff, Arkansas is known as the "World Center of Archery Bow Production."

Heavenly Dove

6 doves, cleaned, dressed
Flour
2 tablespoons (¼ stick) butter
⅛ teaspoon thyme
⅛ teaspoon rosemary
1 teaspoon finely chopped parsley
1 medium onion, finely chopped
1 (4 ounce) can mushrooms with liquid
1 cup sauterne wine
½ teaspoon salt

Cut doves along backbone and butterfly by removing large bones of lower back and legs. Press flat and roll in flour. Brown lightly in butter and sprinkle with herbs and parsley.

Cover and cook slowly for 15 minutes. Add onions, mushrooms with liquid and wine. Cover and simmer for 1 hour or until tender. Add salt 5 minutes before removing from heat. Serve with wild rice or hot buttered rice.

Tip: Quail or squab may be substituted for doves.

Kentucky has more than 1,000,000 acres designated as national parks and recreational areas. The Daniel Boone National Park, Mammoth Cave National Park, Cumberland Gap National Historical Park, the Big South Fork National River and Recreation Area and the Land Between the Lakes include rivers, streams, mountains, lush forests, ancient caves and natural beauty that is some of the most beautiful scenery in the world.

Joe David's Roast Venison

4 pounds venison roast
1 (1 ounce) package dry onion soup mix
¼ cup vinegar
1 tablespoon soy sauce
1 tablespoon Worcestershire sauce
1 large onion, sliced
1 piece suet

Preheat oven to 325°. Wash and trim meat. Soak overnight in salted water to cover. Drain off water and re-soak in salted water.

Trim off shreds of whitish membranes. Sprinkle soup mix into baking pan and add roast.

In bowl, combine vinegar, soy sauce and Worcestershire sauce and spoon over meat. Place onion slices over meat. Cut strips of suet and secure to meat with toothpicks.

Cover pan with heavy aluminum foil and seal edges around lip of pan. Cover loosely to allow space for steam and bake for 4 hours.

The Mississippi Sandhill Crane is about 44 inches tall and has an eight-foot wingspan. It is the rarest of North American cranes and can be found in the grassy savannas of Jackson County, Mississippi.

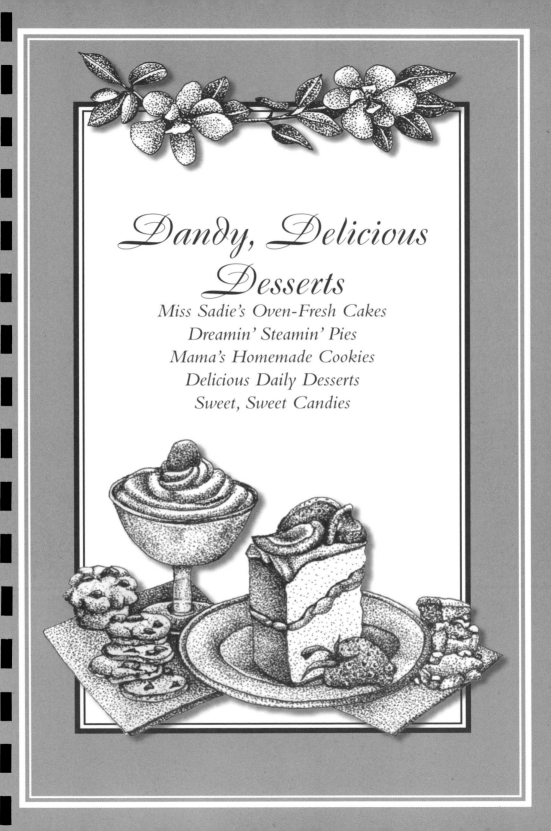

Dandy, Delicious Desserts

Miss Sadie's Oven-Fresh Cakes
Dreamin' Steamin' Pies
Mama's Homemade Cookies
Delicious Daily Desserts
Sweet, Sweet Candies

Apricot-Nectar Cake

The longer this sits, the better it tastes.

Cake:

1 (18 ounce) box lemon cake mix
1 cup apricot nectar
4 eggs
¾ cup oil
½ cup sugar

Preheat oven to 350°. Combine all ingredients and mix well. Bake in greased, floured tube pan for 1 hour. Cool 5 minutes, remove from pan and ice while hot.

Icing:

Juice from 1 lemon
1½ cups powdered sugar

Combine ingredients and pour slowly over hot cake so icing seeps into cake. Spread remaining icing on sides of cake.

Tip: Make recipe the day before you eat so icing has time to seep into cake. It's wonderful and will store just fine.

Lumberton, Mississippi houses the world's largest pecan nursery.

Carrot Cake

2 cups flour, sifted
2 cups sugar
¼ teaspoon salt
1 teaspoon baking powder
1 teaspoon baking soda
1 teaspoon cinnamon
4 eggs
1½ cups vegetable oil
2 cups grated carrots

Preheat oven to 350°. Grease and flour 3 (9-inch) layer cake pans. Sift dry ingredients together. Blend eggs and vegetable oil. Add dry ingredients and mix thoroughly. Stir in carrots. Pour into prepared pans and bake for 30 to 40 minutes.

Icing:

1 (8 ounce) package cream cheese, softened
½ cup (1 stick) butter
1 teaspoon vanilla extract
1 (16 ounce) package powdered sugar
1 cup chopped pecans

Cream together softened cream cheese and butter. Add vanilla and sugar. Frost cake and sprinkle with chopped nuts.

---

*The RC Cola and Moon Pie Festival are
held annually in Bell Buckle, Tennessee.*

Strawberry Cake

1 (18 ounce) box white cake mix
3 teaspoons flour
1 (3 ounce) box strawberry gelatin
1 (10 ounce) package frozen strawberries, thawed,
  divided
½ cup water
1 cup corn oil
4 eggs

Preheat oven to 350°. Grease and flour 2 (8 or 9-inch) layer pans
or grease, flour sides of pans and cut out circle of wax paper to fit
bottom of pan.

Combine cake mix, flour and gelatin and mix well. In small bowl,
mix ¾ cup strawberries, water and corn oil. Add to cake mixture
and blend well.

Add eggs one at a time and beat for 1 minute after each egg. Pour
into prepared pans and bake for 35 minutes.

Icing:

½ cup (1 stick) butter
2½ to 3 cups powdered sugar
2 tablespoons milk
Strawberries

Cream butter and sugar with milk. Add small amount of
remaining strawberries for color. If icing is too thin, add more
sugar. Let chill for several hours before serving.

Fresh Apple Cake

1½ cups oil
2½ cups sugar
1 teaspoon vanilla
3 eggs
3 cups flour
1 teaspoon baking soda
1 tablespoon cinnamon
3 cups apples, pared, cored, chopped
1 cup chopped nuts

Preheat oven to 350°. Grease and flour tube pan and set aside. In bowl, combine sugar, oil and vanilla until smooth and creamy. Add eggs and mix well.

Sift in flour, soda and cinnamon. (Batter will be stiff.) Add apples and nuts to mixture and beat thoroughly. Bake for 1 hour, 30 minutes in prepared tube pan.

Rummy Yum Cake

Cake:

1 cup chopped pecans or walnuts
1 (18 ounce) box yellow cake mix
1 (3 ounce) package vanilla instant pudding mix
½ cup dark rum
4 eggs
½ cup cold water
½ cup oil

Preheat oven to 325°. Grease and flour 10-inch tube or 12-cup bundt pan. Sprinkle nuts in bottom. Mix remaining ingredients and pour over nuts and bake for 1 hour. Cool. Invert cake on serving plate.

Glaze:

½ cup (1 stick) butter
¼ cup water
1 cup sugar
½ cup dark rum

Melt butter in saucepan and stir in water and sugar. Boil for 5 minutes and stir constantly. Remove from heat and add rum. Prick top of cake and drizzle glaze evenly over top and sides. Allow cake to absorb glaze and repeat until glaze is completely used.

Lemon Cake

This is an easy cake to make early in the day. Just don't freeze it.

Cake:

1 (18 ounce) box yellow cake mix
¾ cup water
4 eggs
1 (3 ounce) package lemon gelatin
¾ cup cooking oil

Glaze:

2 cups powdered sugar
1 teaspoon grated lemon rind
Juice of 2 lemons
1 (7 ounce) package flaked coconut

Preheat oven to 350°. Mix cake ingredients as listed and beat until fluffy. Pour into greased, floured 9 x 13-inch pan. Bake for 30 to 35 minutes.

Remove cake from oven and jab with fork at 1-inch intervals to bottom. Spoon glaze mixture over warm cake, sprinkle with coconut and serve warm.

Lemon-Pecan Holiday Cake

1 (1½ ounce) bottle lemon extract
4 cups pecan halves
2 cups (4 sticks) butter
3 cups sugar
3½ cups flour, divided
6 eggs
½ pound candied green pineapple, chopped
½ pound candied red cherries, halved
1½ teaspoons baking powder
½ cup flour

Preheat oven to 275°. Pour lemon extract over pecans in medium bowl, toss and set aside. Grease and flour tube cake pan.

In large mixing bowl, cream butter and sugar until fluffy. Sift 3 cups flour and baking powder in separate bowl. Add eggs to butter-sugar mixture, one at a time, and alternate with flour mixture. With pineapple and cherries cut, add ½ cup flour and mix until flour covers fruit well. Fold in fruit and pecans and pour into prepared tube pan.

Bake for 2 hours, 30 minutes to 2 hours, 45 minutes. Test after 2 hours, 30 minutes for doneness. Cool and remove carefully from pan.

Pecans contain no cholesterol and add essential fiber, vitamin E, magnesium, thiamin and copper to the diet. They are also high in monounsaturated fats that help lower LDL cholesterol blood levels.

Mississippi Mud Cake

2 cups sugar
⅓ cup cocoa
1½ cups (3 sticks) butter
4 eggs
1 teaspoon vanilla extract
1½ cups flour
1⅓ cups flaked coconut
1½ cups chopped pecans
1 (7 ounce) jar marshmallow cream

Preheat oven to 350°. Cream sugar, cocoa, and butter and add eggs and vanilla. Mix well. Stir in flour, coconut, and pecans. Bake in 9 x 13-inch pan for 40 minutes. When done, spread marshmallow cream over hot cake. Cool before frosting.

Icing:

1 (16 ounce) box powdered sugar
½ cup (1 stick) butter, softened
½ cup evaporated milk
⅓ cup cocoa
1 teaspoon vanillas extract

Sift sugar and cocoa. Cream butter with dry ingredients, then stir in milk and vanilla. Spread over cake.

Chocolate Picnic Cake

Cake:

2 cups flour
2 cups sugar
1 cup water
½ cup (1 stick) butter
½ cup shortening
5 tablespoons cocoa
½ cup buttermilk
2 eggs
1 teaspoon baking soda
1 teaspoon vanilla

Preheat oven to 350°. Sift flour and sugar. Cook water, butter, shortening and cocoa until they melt. Cool, pour over flour mixture and mix well.

Add buttermilk, eggs, soda and vanilla and mix well. Pour into sprayed 9 x 13-inch pan and bake for 25 to 35 minutes.

Icing:

½ cup (1 stick) butter
6 tablespoons milk
4 tablespoons cocoa
1 (16 ounce) box powdered sugar
1 teaspoon vanilla
Chopped nuts

Bring butter, milk and cocoa to boil. Remove from heat and add sugar, vanilla and nuts. Pour over hot cake.

Sour Cream-Chocolate Chip Cake
This is so easy!

1 cup (2 sticks) butter
1¼ cups sugar
3 eggs, lightly beaten
1 (8 ounce) carton sour cream
2 cups sifted cake flour
1 teaspoon baking powder
½ teaspoon baking soda
1 teaspoon vanilla
1 (12 ounce) package miniature chocolate chips
1 cup chopped pecans, optional

Preheat oven to 350°. Cream butter and sugar until smooth. Add eggs and sour cream and mix well. Sift flour, soda and baking powder. Add vanilla, chocolate chips and pecans.

Pour into sprayed tube pan and bake for 1 hour.

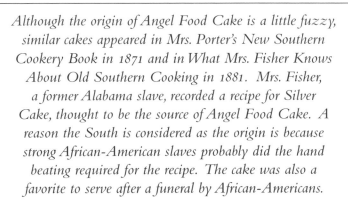

Although the origin of Angel Food Cake is a little fuzzy, similar cakes appeared in Mrs. Porter's New Southern Cookery Book in 1871 and in What Mrs. Fisher Knows About Old Southern Cooking in 1881. Mrs. Fisher, a former Alabama slave, recorded a recipe for Silver Cake, thought to be the source of Angel Food Cake. A reason the South is considered as the origin is because strong African-American slaves probably did the hand beating required for the recipe. The cake was also a favorite to serve after a funeral by African-Americans.

Ashley Baine's Chess Cake

Crust:

1 (18 ounce) box yellow or chocolate cake mix
½ cup (1 stick) butter, softened
1 egg

Preheat oven to 350°. Grease 9 x 13-inch pan. Crumble cake mix, butter and egg. Pat into prepared pan.

Filling:

1 (8 ounce) package cream cheese, softened
1 (16 ounce) package powdered sugar
2 eggs
3 to 4 tablespoons lemon juice for yellow cake or
 coffee for chocolate cake

In mixing bowl, combine cream cheese, sugar, eggs and lemon juice or coffee. Blend thoroughly and pour mixture over crust.

Bake in 350° oven for 35 to 40 minutes or until brown.

Hummingbird Cake

3 cups flour
2 cups sugar
1 teaspoon salt
1 teaspoon cinnamon
1 teaspoon baking soda
3 eggs
1½ cups oil
3 cups mashed bananas
3 cups chopped pecans
1 (8 ounce) can crushed pineapple with juice

Preheat oven to 325°. Sift flour, sugar, salt, cinnamon and baking soda into bowl. Add eggs and oil and mix well with mixer.

Fold in bananas, nuts and pineapple. Bake in large tube pan for 1 hour, 15 minutes. Cool and frost with icing below.

Tip: An alternate method is to bake in 3 (8 or 9-inch) pans at 350° for 25 to 30 minutes.

Cream Cheese Icing:

½ cup (1 stick) butter, softened
1 (8 ounce) package cream cheese, softened
1 (16 ounce) box powdered sugar
1 teaspoon vanilla
1 cup chopped nuts, optional

In bowl, combine butter and cream cheese and beat until smooth. Add powdered sugar and vanilla. Spread over layers, top and sides of cooled cake.

Out-of-This-World Cake

2 cups sugar
1 (2 sticks) cup butter, softened
5 eggs
1 cup milk
1 (13.5 ounce) box graham cracker crumbs
1 tablespoon baking powder
1 (15 ounce) can crushed pineapple, drained
1 (6 ounce) package frozen flaked coconut, thawed
1½ cups chopped nuts
1 tablespoon vanilla

Preheat oven to 350°. Grease and flour tube pan. In bowl, combine all ingredients and mix well using electric mixer.

Pour into prepared pan and bake for about 1 hour, 20 minutes. After about 1 hour, 15 minutes, test with straw for doneness. Set aside to cool before removing from pan.

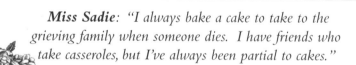

Miss Sadie: "I always bake a cake to take to the grieving family when someone dies. I have friends who take casseroles, but I've always been partial to cakes."

Poppy Seed Cake

3 cups sugar
1¼ cups shortening
6 eggs
3 cups flour
¼ teaspoon baking soda
½ teaspoons salt
1 cup buttermilk
3 tablespoons poppy seeds
2 teaspoons almond extract
2 teaspoons vanilla
2 teaspoons butter flavoring

Glaze:

1½ cups powdered sugar
⅓ cup lemon juice
1 teaspoon vanilla
1 teaspoon almond extract

Preheat oven to 325°. In large mixing bowl, cream sugar and shortening until mixture is light and fluffy. Add eggs, one at a time, and blend mixture well. Sift flour, baking soda and salt.

Alternately add dry ingredients and buttermilk to sugar mixture. Add poppy seeds and flavorings and blend well. Pour into greased, floured bundt pan. Cook for about 1 hour, 15 minutes. Test with toothpick for doneness.

For glaze, combine all ingredients and mix well. Pour over top of cooled cake and let some glaze run down sides of cake.

Praline Cheesecake

1¼ cups graham cracker crumbs
4 tablespoons sugar
¼ cup (½ stick) butter, melted
3 (8 ounce) packages cream cheese, softened
1¼ cups packed dark brown sugar
2 tablespoons flour
3 large eggs
2 teaspoons vanilla
½ cup finely chopped pecans
Pecan halves
Maple syrup

Preheat oven to 350°. Combine crumbs, sugar and butter and press into bottom of 9-inch springform pan. Bake for 10 minutes.

With mixer, combine cream cheese, brown sugar and flour and blend well at medium speed. Add eggs, one at a time, and mix well after each addition. Blend in vanilla, stir in chopped pecans and pour mixture over crust. Bake for 50 to 55 minutes.

Remove from oven and loosen cake from rim of pan. Let cake cool before removing from pan. Chill. Place pecans halves around edge of cake (about 1 inch from edge and 1 inch apart) and pour syrup over top. When you slice cheesecake, pour another tablespoon syrup over each slice so some will run down sides.

ℱestive Christmas Cake

This is easy to make and great if you make the day before.

1 (18 ounce) box lemon supreme pound cake mix
1 (12 ounce) package mixed candied fruit, dredged in
flour

Prepare cake mix according to package directions. Fold in candied fruit into batter before pouring into cake pan. Bake according to package directions. (Some fruit may be reserved for garnish.)

Icing:

3 tablespoons butter, softened
1 cup powdered sugar
1½ tablespoons sherry wine

Cream softened butter and sugar. Add sherry gradually until icing is of spreading consistency. Spread over top of cake and garnish with candied fruit.

Tip: Cut fruit to represent poinsettia, if desired.

The Only Great Pound Cake

½ cup shortening
1 cup (2 sticks) butter
3 cups sugar
5 eggs
3½ cups flour
½ teaspoon baking powder
1 cup milk
1 teaspoon rum flavoring
1 teaspoon coconut flavoring

Glaze:

1 cup sugar
⅓ cup water
½ teaspoon almond extract

Preheat oven to 325°. In mixing bowl, cream shortening, butter and sugar, add eggs and beat for 4 minutes. Combine flour and baking powder and add dry ingredients and milk alternately to butter mixture. Begin and end with flour. Add rum and coconut flavorings.

Pour mixture into large sprayed tube pan and bake for 1 hour, 35 minutes. Test with toothpick. (Do not open door during baking.) Right before cake is done, bring sugar and water to rolling boil. Remove from heat and add almond extract. While cake is still in pan, pour glaze over cake and set aside for 30 minutes before removing from pan.

Easy Pound Cake

2 cups flour
1 cup (2 sticks) butter, softened
5 eggs
2 cups sugar
½ cup milk
2 teaspoons baking powder
1 teaspoon vanilla

Preheat oven to 350°. Spray tube pan. Using mixer, combine all ingredients and mix for 10 minutes at medium speed. Pour into prepared pan and bake for 50 minutes to 1 hour. Cool

---

Pound cakes have been in the South long before the first recorded recipes of the 18th century. They were named Pound Cakes because of the equal weight of each of the ingredients: 1 pound flour, 1 pound butter, 1 pound sugar and 1 pound eggs. In "The Virginia Housewife" published in 1824, Mary Randolph uses these ingredients and measurements and suggests adding grated lemon peel, nutmeg and brandy. She also suggests baking as a cake, as a pudding in a large mold and boiling it and serving with butter and sugar.

Double Chocolate Pound Cake

1 cup (2 sticks) butter, softened
½ cup shortening
1 (3 ounce) package cream cheese, softened
3 cups sugar
2 teaspoons vanilla
5 large eggs
½ cup cocoa
3 cups flour
1 teaspoon baking powder
½ teaspoon salt
1 cup buttermilk
1 (6 ounce) package chocolate chips
Powdered sugar

Preheat oven to 325°. In large mixing bowl, cream butter, shortening, cream cheese and sugar. Beat at high speed for 5 minutes, add vanilla and eggs and beat well. In separate bowl mix cocoa, flour, baking powder and salt. Add half dry ingredients to batter, then buttermilk, and end with remaining dry ingredients. Beat well after each addition. Fold in chocolate chips.

Pour into greased, floured 10-inch tube pan and bake for 1 hour, 30 minutes. Test with toothpick. Cool cake in pan for 15 minutes, turn onto cake plate and cool completely. Dust with sifted powdered sugar.

Sissy's Cream Puff Pie

This recipe gives you the same grandeur of individual cream puffs without the time.

½ cup boiling water
¼ cup shortening
⅛ teaspoon salt
½ cup flour
2 eggs
1 (4 ounce) package instant vanilla pudding
1 cup whipped cream
Strawberries
1 cup whipped topping, optional

Preheat oven to 400°. Spray 9-inch pie plate and set aside. Mix boiling water, shortening and salt over heat. Stir in flour all at once. Stir until mixture pulls away from sides and forms into a ball.

Remove from heat and cool slightly. Beat in eggs, one at a time, until smooth. Spread in prepared pan but not onto sides. Bake for 50 to 60 minutes. Sides will rise up and curl in slightly. Cool slowly away from drafts.

Mix vanilla pudding according to package directions. Fold in whipped cream. Pour cream filling into crust and top with strawberries. Top with additional whipped topping, if desired.

Peach-Mousse Pie

1 (9-inch) graham cracker or cookie piecrust
1 (16 ounce) package frozen peach slices, thawed
1 cup sugar
1 (1 ounce) package unflavored gelatin
⅛ teaspoon ground nutmeg
A few drops of yellow and red food coloring
¾ (12 ounce) carton whipped topping
Nectarine slices for garnish

Place peaches in blender and process until smooth. Place in saucepan, bring to boil and stir constantly. Remove from burner, combine sugar, gelatin and nutmeg and stir into hot puree until sugar and gelatin dissolve.

Pour gelatin mixture into large mixing bowl. Place in freezer for 20 minutes or until mixture mounds. Stir occasionally. Beat mixture at high speed for 5 minutes or until mixture becomes lightly and fluffy. Add coloring, fold in whipped topping and pour into piecrust.

More than 40 varieties of peaches are grown in Georgia and harvested between May and August. Clingstone peaches are great for canning, pickling and eating early in the season, but are not generally used for cooking. Freestone varieties have pits that separate easily from the flesh, making them easy to peel. Varieties that are firm are best for cooking. And, late season varieties are best for jams, jellies and preserves because they have more pectin and natural sugars.

Peach-Parfait Pie

3½ cups sliced peaches
1 (3 ounce) package lemon gelatin
½ cup cold water
1 pint vanilla ice cream
1 (8 ounce) carton whipped topping
1 (9-inch) unbaked piecrust

Sweeten fresh peaches with ½ to ¾ cup sugar or substitute
1 (29 ounce) can sliced peaches for fresh peaches. If you use fresh
peaches, let stand for 15 minutes after mixing with sugar.

Drain peaches, fresh or canned, and set aside syrup. Add water
to syrup to make 1 cup. Heat to boil, add gelatin and stir until it
dissolves. Add cold water.

Spoon ice cream into mixture and stir until it melts. Chill until
mixture mounds slightly when dropped from spoon. Fold in
peaches. Turn into cooled piecrust and chill until firm. Top with
whipped topping and additional peaches, if desired.

*The Elberta Peach is the most widely
planted variety of peaches ever introduced
and is grown in all parts of the world.*

Pineapple-Coconut Pie

1 (9-inch) unbaked deep-dish piecrust
½ cup (1 stick) butter, melted
2 cups sugar
4 eggs, slightly beaten
1 (10 ounce) can flaked coconut
1 (8 ounce) can pineapple chunks, slightly drained

Preheat oven to 350°. Mix all ingredients and pour into
2 unbaked piecrusts. Bake for 45 minutes to 1 hour or until
golden brown.

Virginia is the official birthplace of several U.S. presidents,
including George Washington, Thomas Jefferson, James
Madison, James Monroe, William Henry Harrison,
John Tyler, Zachary Taylor and Woodrow Wilson.

Miss Sadie: *"If you have good manners and keep a*
smile on your face, you'll do just fine in this world."

Strawberry Pie

2 cups sliced strawberries
1 cup sugar
4 tablespoons cornstarch
4 tablespoons strawberry gelatin
1 tablespoon lemon juice, optional
1½ cups water
2 (8 or 9-inch) piecrusts or 1 deep-dish crust, baked
Whipped topping

Combine sugar, cornstarch, gelatin, lemon juice and water, cook until thick and stir occasionally. Cool.

Place berries in piecrusts and pour thickened mixture on top. Chill at least 3 hours. Serve with whipped topping and garnish with halved or whole berries, if desired.

A native wild strawberry grown on the eastern coast called Fragaria Virginiana was the start of today's strawberries grown primarily in California. Cultivation of the wild Virginia strawberry started sometime in the 1600's by Native Americans who introduced them to the colonists.

Company Pumpkin Pie

1 (8 ounce) package cream cheese, softened
¼ cup sugar
½ teaspoon vanilla
1 egg
1 (9-inch) unbaked piecrust
1¼ cups canned pumpkin
½ cup sugar
1 teaspoon cinnamon
¼ teaspoon ginger
¼ teaspoon nutmeg
Dash of salt
1 cup evaporated milk
2 eggs, beaten slightly

Preheat oven to 350°. Mix cream cheese, sugar and vanilla until they blend. Add egg and mix well. Spread into piecrust.

In bowl, combine remaining ingredients and pour over cream cheese mixture. Bake for 65 minutes.

Tip: Protect piecrust by placing 1-inch strip of foil around edges.

Fannie's Pumpkin-Cream Pie

1 (8 ounce) package cream cheese, softened
2½ cups powdered sugar, divided
1 (8 ounce) carton whipped topping
2 (6 ounce) butter-flavored ready piecrusts
¼ cup milk
1 (5 ounce) package instant vanilla pudding
1 (15 ounce) can pumpkin
1 teaspoon cinnamon
½ teaspoon ginger
¼ teaspoon cloves

In mixing bowl, combine cream cheese and 2 cups powdered sugar and beat until smooth and creamy. Fold in whipped topping and pour half cream cheese mixture in each piecrust. In same mixing bowl, combine milk, instant pudding and ½ cup powdered sugar and beat until smooth.

Fold in pumpkin, cinnamon, ginger and cloves. Spread half pumpkin mixture over both pies. Chill for 3 or 4 hours before serving. Eat one pie and freeze the other.

The Edisto River Canoe and Kayak Trail in South Carolina covers 66 miles of the Edisto River. The river is believed to be the world's longest free flowing "black water" stream. The term "black water" describes the water's color and the rate of flow that is characteristic of such rivers.

Macaroon-Crunch Pie

½ cup plus 2 tablespoons shredded coconut, divided
1 (9-inch) baked piecrust
3 cups orange sherbet, softened
1½ cups whipping cream
⅓ cup powdered sugar
1 cup crisp, crushed macaroon cookies
½ cup chopped pecans

Toast ½ cup coconut in shallow pan at 325° for 5 to 10 minutes or until light brown. Stir often to keep from burning. Remove from oven and sprinkle toasted coconut into piecrust. Cover with sherbet and place in freezer.

Beat cream and sugar until thick. Reserve 1 cup for topping. Fold crushed cookies and nuts into remaining cream. Spoon over sherbet and top with whipping cream and 2 tablespoons coconut. Freeze for 6 hours.

Tip: *This pie will store and freeze well. Also, substitute your choice of sherbet flavor.*

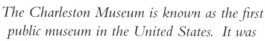

The Charleston Museum is known as the first public museum in the United States. It was founded in 1772 and still operates today.

Peanut Pie

You will need to make this in advance and freeze.

1 (3 ounce) package cream cheese
½ cup smooth peanut butter
1 cup powdered sugar
½ cup milk
1 (8 ounce) container whipped topping
¼ cup finely chopped peanuts
1 (9-inch) graham cracker piecrust
Chopped peanuts for garnish

Blend cream cheese, peanut butter, powdered sugar and milk until smooth. Fold in whipped topping.

Pour into piecrust and top with peanuts. Freeze. Do NOT thaw before cutting and serving pie.

---

*"Goober", meaning peanut, is a derivative
of the African word "nguba" and came to the
U.S. during the African slave trade.*

Willa Mae's Pecan Pie

2 tablespoons flour
3 tablespoons butter, melted
3 eggs, beaten
⅔ cup sugar
1 cup corn syrup
1 teaspoon vanilla
1 cup chopped pecans
1 (9-inch) unbaked piecrust

Preheat oven to 350°. In mixing bowl, combine flour, butter, eggs, sugar, corn syrup and vanilla and mix well. Place pecans in piecrust and pour egg mixture over pecans. Bake for 10 minutes, reduce heat to 275° and bake another 50 to 55 minutes or until center of pie is firm.

Tip: Protect piecrust by placing 1-inch strip of foil around edges.

Pecans are extremely populated in the South and are used in appetizers, salads, vegetables, main dishes and desserts. Pecans add flavor, texture and crunch to many Southern favorites.

Southern Whiskey Pie

5 eggs
1¾ cups sugar
1 tablespoon vinegar
4 tablespoons bourbon
⅓ cup (¾ stick) butter, melted
1 (9-inch) unbaked piecrust

Preheat oven to 325°. Beat eggs until light and gradually add sugar. Stir in vinegar, bourbon and melted butter and mix well. Pour into piecrust and bake for 35 minutes until light brown on top. Serve warm or at room temperature.

Tip: You can place strips of foil over piecrust edges to prevent it from browning too much.

Kentucky is known today as the Bluegrass State. The grass is not really blue; it is green. However in the spring it produces bluish-purple buds that give the grass a blue cast when seen growing in large fields.

Lemon-Pecan Chess Pie

2¼ cups sugar
2 tablespoons flour
1 tablespoon cornmeal
4 eggs, lightly beaten
2 tablespoons grated lemon rind
¼ cup lemon juice
¾ cup chopped pecans
1 (9-inch) unbaked piecrust

Preheat oven to 400°. Combine sugar, flour and cornmeal in large bowl and toss lightly. Add eggs, lemon rind and lemon juice and mix until smooth and it blends thoroughly. Add pecans to mixture and pour into piecrust. Bake for 10 minutes. Turn oven temperature down to 325° and bake another 40 to 45 minutes or until center is not shaky.

Tip: Cover piecrust edges with strips of foil to prevent excessive browning.

*The origin of chess pie is probably England. Settlers
who made it a specialty brought it to the South.
Today, the South claims to be its true home.*

Sunny Lemon Chess Pie

1 (9-inch) unbaked piecrust
3 tablespoons corn meal
2 cups sugar
¼ cup (½ stick) plus 1 tablespoon butter, melted
4 eggs, slightly beaten
¼ cup lemon juice
½ teaspoon lemon zest

Preheat oven at 350°. In bowl, combine all ingredients and mix well. Pour mixture into piecrust and bake for 45 minutes or until center is set and brown on top.

Chess pies are Southern specialties dating back to African-American cooks on southern plantations. They are a simple mixture of sugar, butter, eggs and a little flour with variations of flavorings such as lemon, vanilla and chocolate.

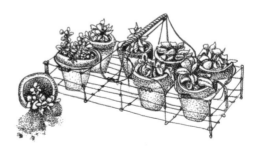

Chocolate Chess Pie

1 (8 or 9-inch) unbaked piecrust
½ cup (1 stick) butter
1 (1 ounce) square unsweetened chocolate
1 cup sugar
2 eggs
Dash salt
1 teaspoon vanilla
Whipped cream
½ cup nuts, optional

Preheat oven to 450°. If desired, bake crust for about
5 minutes. Remove crust from oven and reduce heat to 350°.

Melt butter and chocolate in double boiler. Blend remaining
ingredients, except whipped cream and nuts, and thoroughly
combine with melted butter and chocolate.

Pour into piecrust and bake for 25 to 30 minutes. Top with
whipped cream and nuts.

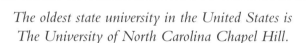

*The oldest state university in the United States is
The University of North Carolina Chapel Hill.*

Chocolate-Angel Pie

2 egg whites
⅛ teaspoon cream of tartar
⅛ teaspoon salt
½ cup sugar
½ cup finely chopped walnuts or pecans
½ teaspoon vanilla
4 (1 ounce) packages German sweet chocolate
3 tablespoons water
1 teaspoon vanilla
1 (8 ounce) carton whipping cream, whipped

Preheat oven to 325°. Beat egg whites with salt and cream of tartar until foamy. Add sugar gradually, beating until very stiff peak holds. Fold in nuts and ½ teaspoon vanilla.

Spread in sprayed 8 or 9-inch pie plate or into 8 individual pie shells. Build up sides to ½-inch above pan. Bake for 50 to 55 minutes. Cool.

Melt chocolate and water in double boiler over low heat and stir constantly. Cool until thick. Add vanilla and fold into whipped cream. Pile into meringue shell. Chill at least 2 hours before serving.

Tip: You can prepare this recipe 1 to 2 days ahead.

> *The Furniture Capital of the World is known*
> *as High Point, North Carolina. It is home to*
> *the International Home Furnishings Market*
> *held annually in April and October.*

Mississippi Mud Pie

4 ounces chocolate wafers
½ cup (1 stick) butter
1 quart coffee ice cream
1½ cups chocolate fudge ice cream sauce
Whipped topping
Sliced almonds

Process wafers to crumbs. Melt butter in saucepan, add wafer crumbs and stir well. Press buttered, wafer crumbs in bottom and sides of 9-inch pie plate and cool.

Soften ice cream and spread on top of wafer crust. Freeze several hours or until firm. Spread fudge sauce over top and freeze overnight. Serve with whipped topping and garnish with sliced almonds.

For decades, chocolate, cake and pudding has been combined in several different ways. The history of the Mississippi Mud Cake or Mississippi Mud Pie is uncertain; however, we do know that both gained national fame and spread from its Southern roots sometime after World War II. It is believed to have begun in the Vicksburg-Natchez area, as the original cake resembled the muddy banks of the Mississippi River. It had layers of chocolate cake and pudding, topped with chocolate icing that looked crusted and cracked similar to the riverbanks in the hot summertime.

Chocolate-Meringue Pie

2 eggs, separated
2 cups milk, divided
½ cup sugar
⅓ cup self-rising flour
¼ teaspoon salt
2 tablespoons (¼ stick) butter
¾ teaspoon vanilla
1 (8-inch) baked piecrust
½ cup semi-sweet chocolate morsels
½ cup pecans pieces

In top of double boiler, mix egg yolks with ¼ cup milk. Add sugar, flour and salt and mix thoroughly. Add remaining milk.

Cook over boiling water about 6 to 7 minutes and stir constantly until thick. Cover and cook 5 minutes longer.

Remove from boiling water and stir in butter and vanilla. Pour into piecrust and sprinkle morsels and pecans over filling.

Meringue:

2 egg whites
¼ cup sugar

Preheat oven to 425°. Beat egg whites until foamy. Add sugar until meringue forms stiff peaks. Spread over pie and bake for 10 minutes or until light brown.

Tip: To keep crust crisp, do not refrigerate unless necessary.

Betty Gail's Brownie Pie

Really a special treat!

1 cup sugar
½ cup flour
2 eggs, beaten slightly
½ cup (1 stick) butter, melted
1 cup chopped pecans
1 cup chocolate chips
1 teaspoon vanilla
Whipped topping
1 (9-inch) unbaked piecrust

Preheat oven to 350°. Mix sugar and flour and add eggs. Add slightly cooled, melted butter and mix well. Add pecans, chocolate chips and vanilla and pour into unbaked piecrust.

Bake for 45 minutes and top with whipped topping.

Sinful Sundae Pie

You must do this ahead of time so it will freeze.

1 cup evaporated milk
1 (6 ounce) package semi-sweet chocolate pieces
¼ teaspoon salt
1 cup miniature marshmallows
1 quart vanilla ice cream
1 (9-inch) vanilla wafer crumb crust
Walnut or almond, slivered

Combine milk, chocolate and salt in saucepan. Stir over LOW heat until mixture melts and is thick. Remove from heat and add marshmallows. Stir until they melt and are smooth. Cool to room temperature.

Spoon half ice cream into crust. Cover with half chocolate mixture. Repeat with remaining ingredients. Garnish with nuts and freeze until firm, at least 5 hours.

Vanilla Wafer Crumb Crust:

1½ cups vanilla wafer crumbs
¼ cup (½ stick) butter

Preheat oven to 350°. Mix ingredients well and bake for 10 minutes. Cool.

Edna Mae's Chocolate Pie

¾ cup sugar
3 tablespoons flour
¼ cup (½ stick) butter
¼ teaspoon salt
3 egg yolks, beaten
1 (13 ounce) can evaporated milk
5½ ounces chocolate syrup
1 tablespoon vanilla
1 (9-inch) baked piecrust
Whipped cream or whipped topping

Mix sugar and flour in saucepan. Add butter, salt, beaten egg yolks, evaporated milk, chocolate syrup and vanilla. Stir until all ingredients are moist.

Bring to boil over medium heat and cook 8 to 10 minutes. Stir constantly. Cool and stir several times. Pour into prepared piecrust. Top with whipped cream or whipped topping. Garnish with shaved chocolate, if desired.

The Great Smoky Mountains National Park was named for the smoke-like blue haze often enveloping the mountains. It is the most visited national park in the United States.

German Chocolate Pie

This is so easy and you can make it ahead of time and freeze.

3 cups granulated sugar
Pinch of salt
7 tablespoons cocoa
4 eggs, beaten
1 teaspoon vanilla
1 (13 ounce) can evaporated milk
½ cup (1 stick) butter
2 cups flaked coconut
1 cup chopped nuts, optional
2 (9-inch) unbaked piecrusts

Preheat oven to 350°. Mix sugar, salt and cocoa. Add eggs and mix well. Stir in vanilla and milk. Add melted butter, coconut and nuts.

Pour into unbaked piecrusts. Bake for 40 minutes or until firm.

The New Madrid Earthquake occurred sometime during the winter of 1811 or 1812 in northwestern Tennessee. It was the largest earthquake in American history. Reelfoot Lake in Obion and Lake Counties was formed as a result of the earthquake.

Peach Fried Pies

Filling:

1 (8 ounce) package dried peaches
1 cup sugar

Crust:

4 cups sifted flour
½ teaspoon salt
1 cup shortening
1 cup ice water

Rinse peaches and place in large pot. Barely cover with cold water, cover and simmer over low heat until tender. Mash peaches, add sugar and blend well. Cool completely.

To prepare crust, cut shortening into flour and add salt until crumbly. Gradually add water and work together using fingers. Roll out on floured board to ⅛-inch thickness. Cut in 3½-inch circles and roll each circle again slightly for thinner edge.

Place 1 heaping teaspoon of filling in each circle. Fold circle in half (use ice water to help seal edges together). In large skillet with ⅓-inch melted shortening, fry both sides of pies until golden brown. Remove to paper towels and drain. Sprinkle powdered sugar over top while hot.

Tip: Substitute dried apples or dried apricots for peaches.

Quick and Easy Peach Cobbler

1 (20 ounce) can peach pie filling
1 (20 ounce) can crushed pineapple with juice
1 cup chopped pecans
1 (18 ounce) box yellow cake mix
1 cup (2 sticks) butter, melted

Pour and pie filling into sprayed 9 x 13-inch baking dish and spread evenly.

Spoon pineapple and juice over pie filling. Sprinkle pecans over pineapple and then sprinkle cake mix over pecans. Drizzle melted butter over cake mix.

Bake at 375° for 40 minutes or until light brown and crunchy. Serve hot or at room temperature with whipped topping or ice cream.

Tip: For variety, substitute apricot pie filling for the peach.

Peaches are a great source of vitamin C and fiber.
One peach provides 10% of the daily requirement of
vitamin C and 8% of the daily requirement of fiber.

Date-Pecan Tarts

1 (8 ounce) package chopped dates
2½ cups milk
½ cups flour
1½ cups sugar
3 eggs
½ teaspoon salt
1 teaspoon vanilla
1 cup chopped pecans
8 tart shells, baked, cooled
1 (8 ounce) carton whipping cream
3 tablespoons powdered sugar

In saucepan, cook dates, milk, flour and sugar until thick and stir constantly. Add beaten eggs and salt. Cook this mixture for 5 minutes on medium heat and stir constantly.

Stir in vanilla and pecans and pour into tart shells. Cool, whip cream and add powdered sugar. Top each tart with a heaping tablespoon whipped cream.

Shelled pecans may be stored in the refrigerator for 9 months maximum. If stored in sealed freezer bags, pecans may keep for up to 2 years. Unshelled pecans may be stored in an airtight container in a dry, cool place for up to 6 months.

Mincemeat

3 pounds lean beef (round steak), boiled
1 pound suet
2 pounds raisins, seeded or seedless
½ pound citron
Juice and grated rind of 1½ lemons
Juice and grated rind of 1½ oranges
½ peck (6 pounds) apples
½ teaspoon salt
2 cups white sugar
2¼ cups packed brown sugar
1¼ quarts apple cider
½ teaspoon pepper
1 teaspoon ginger
2 teaspoons cinnamon
1 teaspoon cloves
2 teaspoons allspice
1 teaspoon nutmeg
Sherry to taste

Grind cooked lean beef, suet, raisins and citron. Place in large pan or tub. Add lemon and orange juice and rind. Clean grinder before grinding and add peeled, cored apples.

Add salt, sugars, cider, pepper and spices and mix well. Add ½ to 1 cup sherry according to taste. Cover and place in cool (50°) place to "age." Allow at least 2 weeks to "age." Check temperature daily and add sherry to suit your own taste.

When "aging" is complete, package in quart-size containers in refrigerator or freezer until ready to make into pies. Begin shortly after Thanksgiving and your mincemeat will be ready in time for Christmas pies.

Favorite Chocolate Chip Cookies

½ cup (1 stick) butter, softened
¾ cup sugar
¾ cup packed brown sugar
1 egg
1 tablespoon water
½ teaspoon vanilla
1 cup flour
½ teaspoon baking soda
1½ cups quick-cooking oats
1 (6 ounce) package chocolate chips
½ cup chopped pecans

Preheat oven to 350°. In mixing bowl, combine butter, both sugars, egg, water and vanilla and beat well. Add dry ingredients and mix well.

Add oats, chocolate chips and pecans and mix well. Drop by teaspoonfuls onto baking sheet and bake for 12 to 15 minutes or until light brown.

Pecan Drops

This is another of the easy cookie recipes you can whip up in a jiffy.

½ cup (1 stick) butter, softened
½ cup plus 2 tablespoons shortening
1 cup powdered sugar
2½ cups sifted cake flour
2 teaspoons vanilla
1 cup chopped pecans

Preheat oven to 325°. Cream butter and shortening until smooth. Beat in sugar gradually. Stir in flour thoroughly and add vanilla and pecans.

Drop by teaspoonfuls onto ungreased baking sheet. Bake for 15 to 20 minutes or until delicate light brown.

Pecans are native to the Mississippi Valley of the U.S. Lumberton, Mississippi houses the world's largest pecan nursery.

Miss Sadie: *"Honey, don't forget to write your "thank you" notes. When someone is thoughtful enough to do something nice for you, you should be thoughtful enough to thank them properly."*

Shortbread Crunchies

1 cup (2 sticks) butter, softened
1 cup oil
1 cup sugar
1 cup packed brown sugar
1 egg
1 teaspoon vanilla
1 cup quick-cooking oats
3½ cups sifted flour
1 teaspoon baking soda
1 teaspoon salt
1 cup crushed cornflakes
1 (3½ ounce) can flaked coconut
1 cup chopped pecans

Preheat oven to 350°. Cream butter, oil and sugars, then add egg and vanilla and mix well. Add oats and dry ingredients and mix. Add cornflakes, coconut and pecans last and mix. Drop by teaspoons on ungreased baking sheet. Flatten with fork dipped in water and bake for 15 minutes or until only slightly brown.

The Mississippi River's nickname is "Old Man River" and is the largest river in the United States as well as the nation's chief waterway.

Miss Sadie: *"As my mother told me, I'll tell you. 'Bosom your cards, honey.' Nobody needs to know what you know."*

Christmas Cookies

1 cup (2 sticks) butter, softened
1½ cups sugar
¼ teaspoon nutmeg
1 teaspoon vanilla
3 eggs
1 teaspoon baking soda
2½ cups flour
1½ cups raisins, optional
1½ cups chopped pecans
2 cups chopped dates
1 cup candied pineapple
1 cup candied cherries

Preheat oven to 350°. Grease baking sheets. With mixer, cream butter and sugar. Add nutmeg, vanilla, eggs, soda and flour and mix well.

Mix nuts with fruit with large spoon and add to batter. Drop by teaspoon on baking sheet and bake for 12 minutes or until done.

The world's longest cave is Mammoth Cave. It was first promoted in 1816 and is the second oldest tourist attraction in the United States.

All-Kids Peanut Butter Cookies

½ cup (1 stick) butter, softened
¼ cup shortening
⅔ cup sugar
1 cup packed brown sugar
1 egg
1 cup crunchy peanut butter
1¾ cups flour
½ teaspoon baking powder
¾ teaspoon baking soda
¼ teaspoon salt

Preheat oven to 350°. In mixing bowl, cream butter, shortening, both sugars and egg and beat well. Add peanut butter and mix. Add all dry ingredients and mix well.

Using small cookie scoop, place cookies onto ungreased baking sheet. Use fork to flatten cookies and criss-cross fork twice. Bake for 12 minutes. Store covered.

Peanut butter cookies probably originated with George Washington Carver, a scientist from Alabama Tuskegee Institute who developed hundreds of uses for peanuts. In 1916 he wrote a paper listing 105 ways to prepare peanuts for human consumption and included three recipes for peanut cookies with chopped or crushed peanuts.

Peanut Krispies

½ cup (1 stick) butter
2 cups peanut butter
1 (16 ounce) box powdered sugar
3½ cups Rice Krispie cereal
¾ cup chopped peanuts

In large saucepan, melt butter. Add peanut butter and powdered sugar and mix well. Add cereal and peanuts and mix well. Drop by teaspoonfuls onto wax paper.

Potato Chip Cookies

Freeze these if you want to eat them in several weeks.

1 cup (2 sticks) butter, softened
½ cup sugar
1½ to 2 cups flour
1 teaspoon vanilla
½ cup finely chopped pecans, optional
½ cup crushed potato chips
4 tablespoons powdered sugar

Preheat oven to 350°. Cream butter, sugar, flour and vanilla well. Add nuts, stir and add potato chips.

Pinch into marble-sized pieces and place on baking sheet. Press flat with fork. Bake for 13 minutes and sprinkle with powdered sugar.

Advent Spice Cookies

This recipe is easily doubled. It's so good!

¾ cup shortening
1 cup packed brown sugar
1 egg
¼ cup molasses
2¼ cups sifted flour
2 teaspoons baking soda
¼ teaspoon salt
½ teaspoon ground cloves
1 teaspoon cinnamon
1 teaspoon ginger
Extra granulated sugar

Preheat oven to 375°. Thoroughly mix shortening, sugar, egg and molasses. Sift remaining ingredients and stir into first mixture.

Chill dough and shape into large marble-sized balls. Roll in sugar and place balls about 2 inches apart on sprayed baking sheet. Bake for 10 to 12 minutes. Cool for 2 minutes on baking sheet.

Arkansas was the first state to require teachers to pass a basic skills test in 1983.

Orange Balls

*There's nothing hard about these delicious cookies
and they will keep for several weeks.*

1 (12 ounce) box vanilla wafers, crushed
½ cup orange juice concentrate, thawed
1 cup powdered sugar
¾ cup shredded coconut
½ cup chopped pecans
Additional powdered sugar

In bowl, combine all ingredients. Blend mixture well and shape
into balls and store in covered container. Before serving, roll in
additional powdered sugar.

---

*One of the few remaining free-flowing rivers
in the lower 48 states, is the Buffalo National
River. It cuts through massive limestone bluffs
as it flows through the Ozark Mountains.*

Bourbon Balls

1 (6 ounce) package chocolate bits
½ cup granulated sugar
3 tablespoons light corn syrup
½ cup bourbon
2½ cups finely crushed vanilla wafers
1 cup finely chopped nuts
Sifted powdered sugar

Melt chocolate in top of double boiler. Remove from heat and stir in sugar and corn syrup. Add bourbon and blend well.

Combine vanilla wafers and nuts in large bowl. Add chocolate mixture and blend well. If mixture is too sticky, add a few more crushed vanilla wafers. Form into 1-inch balls and roll in powdered sugar. Place in airtight can for 3 days.

Tip: These keep very well so they are good ones to make in advance.

In the late 1780's, Reverend Elijah Craig, a
Baptist minister, developed corn liquor or bourbon
whiskey in Scott County, Kentucky.

Rum Balls

This is so easy!

½ pound vanilla wafers
1 cup plus 4 tablespoons powdered sugar, divided
2 tablespoons cocoa
1 cup finely chopped pecans
½ cup light corn syrup
¼ cup rum or bourbon

Roll vanilla wafers into fine crumbs with rolling pin. Mix all ingredients, except 4 tablespoons powdered sugar, and set aside for 1 hour.

Coat hands with remaining powdered sugar and shape mixture into 1-inch balls. Before serving, roll in powdered sugar.

Nowhere in Kentucky is the feeling of the Old South more obvious than My Old Kentucky Home State Park. Made famous by Stephen Foster's song, the home of John Rowan built in 1818, has been preserved much as was when Stephen Foster visited there.

Almond-Fudge Shortbread

1 cup (2 sticks) butter, softened
1 cup powdered sugar
¼ teaspoon salt
1¼ cups flour
1 (12 ounce) package chocolate chips
1 (14 ounce) can sweetened, condensed milk
½ teaspoon almond extract
1 (2½ ounce) package almonds, toasted

Preheat oven to 350°. Spray 9 x 13-inch baking pan. In mixing bowl, beat butter, sugar and salt and stir in flour. Pat into prepared pan and bake for 15 minutes.

In medium saucepan over low heat, melt chocolate chips with condensed milk and stir constantly until chips melt. Stir in almond extract and spread evenly over shortbread. Sprinkle with almonds. Chill several hours or until firm and cut into bars. They may be stored at room temperature.

The Kentucky Derby is one of the best-known sporting events in the U.S. and is called the "greatest two minutes in sports". The race is for three-year-olds and run on a 1.25 mile track. The race is the premier event in a 2-week schedule of parties, parades, picnics and fireworks. Meriwether Lewis Clark first organized the race in 1875.

Chocolate-Caramel Bars

Truly unusual and delicious!

1 (14 ounce) bag light caramels (about 50 pieces)
1 (5 ounce) can evaporated milk
1 (18 ounce) German chocolate cake mix, divided
¾ cup (½ sticks) butter, melted
1 cup chopped nuts
1 cup chocolate chips

Preheat oven to 350°. Spray 9 x 13-inch baking dish with non-stick spray. Melt caramels and ⅓ cup milk in double boiler.

Combine cake mix, melted butter and remaining ⅓ cup milk and mix well. Spread half cake mixture in prepared baking dish. Bake for 6 minutes and remove from oven.

Sprinkle with nuts and chocolate chips and spread caramel mixture on top. Spread remainder of cake mixture and bake for 15 to 18 minutes. Remove from oven and cool before cutting into bars.

Tip: If you use cake mix with pudding, bake 18 to 20 minutes.

Europeans first landed in Maryland in 1631. During the 17th century it was known as the "Athens of America" and once served as the capital of the U.S. In the 18th century Baltimore Harbor was home to large clipper ships built nearby.

Magic Cookie Bars

These easy bars can be mixed in baking pan for easy clean-up.

1½ cups corn flake crumbs
3 tablespoons sugar
½ cup (1 stick) butter, melted
1 cup coarsely chopped walnuts or pecans
1 (6 ounce) package semi-sweet chocolate morsels
1⅓ cups flaked coconut
1 (14 ounce) can sweetened, condensed milk

Preheat oven to 350°. Combine corn flake crumbs, sugar, and butter and mix thoroughly. Pour mixture into 9 x 13-inch baking pan. With back of tablespoon, press mixture evenly and firmly in bottom of pan to form crust.

Sprinkle nuts, chocolate morsels and coconut evenly over crumb crust. Pour condensed milk evenly over nuts and bake for 25 minutes or until light brown around edges. Cool and cut into bars.

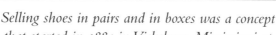

Selling shoes in pairs and in boxes was a concept
that started in 1884 in Vicksburg, Mississippi at
Phil Gilbert's Shoe Parlor on Washington Street.

Oatmeal Crispies

1 cup (2 sticks) butter, softened
1 cup packed brown sugar
1 cup granulated sugar
2 eggs, beaten
1 teaspoon vanilla
1½ cups flour
1 teaspoon salt
1 teaspoon baking soda
3 cups quick oats
½ cup chopped nuts
1 teaspoon cinnamon, optional

Preheat oven to 350°. Cream butter and sugars, add eggs and vanilla and mix well. Sift flour, salt and baking soda and add to batter. Add oats and nuts. Add cinnamon if desired. Shape into rolls and wrap in wax paper. Chill.

Line baking sheets with foil or spray pan and set aside. Slice cookies, place on sheets and dip in extra granulated sugar for a different taste. Bake for 8 to 12 minutes.

Tip: These are so easy and they made be halved and frozen. Freeze dough in rolls and slice while still frozen.

Ice Box Cookies

1 cup shortening
¼ cup packed brown sugar
1 cup sugar
1 egg
¼ teaspoon salt
1½ teaspoons vanilla
2 cups flour
2 teaspoons baking powder
1 cup chopped pecans

Preheat oven to 350°. Combine shortening, both sugars, egg, salt and vanilla and mix well. Add flour and baking powder and mix until it blends well. Add pecans and mix. Divide dough in half and roll in log shape on wax paper. Roll remaining half in another log. Chill for several hours.

Slice into ¼-inch slices. Place on baking sheet and bake for 15 minutes or until slightly brown.

More than 500 buildings in Natchez, Mississippi are
listed in the National Register of Historic Places.

Blonde Brownies

These are unbelievably delicious, so easy, store
well and you can even freeze them.

1 cup (2 sticks) butter
1 (16 ounce) box light brown sugar
2 eggs
2 cups flour
2 teaspoons baking powder
1 teaspoon vanilla extract
Pinch of salt
1 cup chopped pecans

Preheat oven to 350°. Melt butter in heavy saucepan. Add sugar and stir in eggs, flour and baking powder. Add vanilla, salt and pecans. Bake in sprayed 9 x 13–inch pan for 25 minutes.

The Okefenokee Swamp in Georgia provides sanctuaries
for hundreds of bird species and wildlife including
endangered species. It encompasses over 400,000 acres of
canals, moss-draped cypress trees and lily pad prairies.

Hello Dollies

½ cup (1 stick) butter
1 cup graham cracker crumbs
1 (3½ ounce) package flaked coconut
1 (6 ounce bag) butterscotch chips
1 (6 ounce) bag chocolate chips
1 cup pecan pieces
1 (14 ounce) can sweetened, condensed milk

Preheat oven to 350°. Melt butter in 9 x 9-inch pan. Spread crumbs in bottom of pan over butter. Layer coconut, butterscotch chips, chocolate chips and pecans.

Pour condensed milk over top and bake for 30 minutes. Corners will brown. Cool and cut into squares.

Blackbeard Island, Georgia was the home of the pirate Edward "Blackbeard" Teach. The United States Congress designated the Blackbeard Island Wilderness Area in 1975, now totaling 3,000 acres.

Miss Sadie: *"Honey, the family and the home are the most important things in the world. You take good care of 'em now and go bake some cookies."*

Toffee Squares

1 cup (2 sticks) plus 2 tablespoons (¼ stick) butter, softened
1 cup packed brown sugar
1 egg yolk
1 teaspoon vanilla
2 cups flour
1 (8 ounce) chocolate bar
1 cup chopped nuts

Preheat oven to 350°. Cream 1 cup butter and sugar until light. Add beaten egg yolk, vanilla and flour.

Spread thin on baking sheet and bake for 15 to 20 minutes. Cool slightly. Melt chocolate with 2 tablespoons (¼ stick) butter in double boiler and spread on cookie surface. Sprinkle with nuts and cut into squares.

> *The first constitution ever written by white men in America was in 1772 and drafted by the Watauga Association at Sycamore Shoals, Tennessee near Elizabethton. It was patterned after the constitution of the Iroquois League of Nations, a federal system of government developed 200 years earlier for five eastern Native American tribes.*

Ellie's Easy Apple Crisp

You will love making this quick and easy dessert.

2 (20 ounce) cans apple pie filling
Lemon juice
Cinnamon
1 (18 ounce) box yellow cake mix
1 cup chopped walnuts
1 cup (2 sticks) butter, melted

Preheat oven to 350°. Spray 9 x 13-inch baking pan. Pour apples into pan and squeeze small amount of lemon juice over apples. Sprinkle generously with cinnamon. Add cake mix over apples and more cinnamon. Spread walnuts on top and pour melted butter over entire mixture. Bake for 1 hour.

Serve hot, plain or with ice cream or whipped cream.

Two Louisville, Kentucky sisters created the song, "Happy Birthday to You", in 1893.

Cherry Crunch

1 (20 ounce) can cherry pie filling
1 (20 ounce) can crushed pineapple with juice
1 (18 ounce) box yellow cake mix
1 cup (2 sticks) butter
½ cup chopped pecans

Preheat oven to 350°. Spray 9 x 13-inch baking dish. Combine pie filling and pineapple and mix well. Pour in baking dish and sprinkle dry cake mix over mixture.

Melt butter and pour evenly over cake. Bake for 30 minutes, remove from oven and sprinkle pecans over top. Return to oven for 30 more minutes.

Let stand at room temperature for at least 20 minutes before serving.

The first observance of Mother's Day was by Mary S. Wilson, a teacher, in 1887. It became a national holiday in 1916.

Curried Fruit

Delicious with ham, lamb or poultry!

1 (16 ounce) can peach halves
1 (20 ounce) can pineapple slices
1 (16 ounce) can pear halves
5 maraschino cherries
¾ cup packed light brown sugar
2 to 4 teaspoons curry powder
⅓ cup (⅔ stick) butter

Preheat oven to 325°. Drain fruit and dry on paper towels. Arrange fruit in 1½-quart baking dish. Melt butter, add brown sugar and curry powder. Spoon mixture over fruit.

Bake uncovered for 1 hour and chill. Reheat at 350° for 30 minutes before serving.

Mrs. Mamie Thomas was the first female rural mail carrier in the United States. She delivered mail by buggy to areas southeast of Vicksburg, Mississippi in 1914.

Hot Fruit Casserole

1 (16 ounce) can peaches
1 (16 ounce) can pineapple chunks
1 (16 ounce) can pear halves
1 (14 ounce) jar apple rings
2 tablespoons cornstarch
½ cup packed brown sugar
½ cup sherry
¼ cup (½ stick) butter

Preheat oven to 350°. Drain fruit and save juice from peaches, pineapple and apple rings to make 2 cups. Add cornstarch, sugar, sherry and butter to juice and cook until thick.

Arrange fruit attractively in long baking dish. Pour thickened sauce over casserole and bake for 20 minutes. Serve with any meat.

The first attempt to colonize America by English-speaking people was in Coastal North Carolina. Two colonies were started in the 1580's under charter granted by Queen Elizabeth to Sir Walter Raleigh. The first colony was established under the leadership of Ralph Lane in 1585 but ended in failure.

Weezie's Peach Crisp
You will love this easy, peachy dish.

1½ quarts peaches, peeled, sliced
½ cup sugar
Lemon juice
Nutmeg
Cinnamon
½ cup (1 stick) butter, melted
¾ cup self-rising flour
1 cup sugar

Preheat oven to 350°. Arrange peaches and sugar in 3-quart baking dish. Sprinkle lemon juice, nutmeg and cinnamon as desired.

Mix butter, flour and sugar and spread topping over peaches. Bake for 30 to 35 minutes or until brown. Serve plain or with whipped cream or ice cream.

Tip: Apples may be substituted for peaches. If used, substitute orange juice for water.

1 pound fresh peaches = 3 medium peaches
= 2 cups sliced = 1½ cups peach puree.

Orange-Spiced Peaches

1 (28 ounce) can peach halves, with juice
1 teaspoon whole cloves
6 sticks cinnamon
10 whole allspice
½ cup vinegar
⅔ cup sugar
1 orange, sliced

Drain peaches reserving ½ cup syrup. Tie cloves, cinnamon and allspice in small piece of cheesecloth.

In large saucepan, combine vinegar, sugar and orange slices. Add drained peach halves, reserved peach syrup, and spice bag. Heat ingredients to boil, reduce heat and simmer uncovered for 5 minutes.

Cover and let cool to room temperature. Remove spice bag and serve peach halves with orange slice. Serve warm or cold.

The Georgia peach industry was established in 1880 when Samuel H. Rumph began shipping peaches to New York. He created the Elberta Peach, was the first to recognize peaches as a cash crop, planted the first commercial orchard and pioneered refrigerated shipping.

Peach Sauce

6 cups fresh peaches, peeled, sliced
1 cup water
¾ cup sugar
¼ teaspoon ground cinnamon

In large saucepan, combine peaches and water and cook over medium heat for 10 minutes. Reduce heat, cover and simmer another 10 minutes. Cool.

In blender, combine peaches, sugar and cinnamon and process until smooth and creamy. Pour mixture into pint-jar and chill. Serve over pound cake or ice cream.

Charlotte Russe

1 tablespoon unflavored gelatin
½ cup milk, warm
1 (8 ounce) carton whipping cream
¼ cup sugar
½ jigger brandy
Ladyfingers or pound cake

Dissolve gelatin in warm milk and cool slightly. Whip cream and add sugar and brandy. Fold whipped cream mixture into gelatin mixture and pour into dish lined with ladyfingers or thinly sliced pound cake. Chill for 3 to 4 hours or until well set.

Chocolate Leaves

4 ounces semi-sweet chocolate pieces
Non-poisonous leaves

Melt chocolate. Wash leaves. Brush melted chocolate on backs of leaves with ½-inch artist brush. Put in freezer for 2 to 3 minutes or until hard enough to peel leaf from chocolate.

Place chocolate leaves into plastic bag with air in it to cushion leaves. Keep chilled until needed. To keep leaves for longer time, use 6 ounces melted semi-sweet chocolate combined with block of melted paraffin and follow preceding directions.

Tip: A camellia leaf is a good choice because of its size.

Traditional Custard

1 tablespoon flour
1 cup sugar
5 whole eggs
1 gallon milk
1 teaspoon vanilla

In bowl, combine flour and sugar and stir. In separate bowl, beat eggs well and add milk. Combine with flour-sugar mixture and stir until sugar dissolves.

Pour mixture in double boiler, stir constantly and cook until thick. Remove from heat, stir in vanilla and pour into custard cups.

Mother's Boiled Custard

1 gallon milk
½ cup sugar
Dash of salt
4 eggs, slightly beaten
2 teaspoons vanilla

In bowl, combine sugar, salt and eggs and mix well.

In double boiler, scald milk and add a little into egg mixture.
Pour egg-milk mixture into double boiler and cook. Stir
constantly until mixture is thick enough to coat spoon. Remove
from heat and add vanilla. Chill.

Creamy Banana Pudding

1 (14 ounce) can sweetened, condensed milk
1½ cups cold water
1 (3¾ ounce) package instant vanilla pudding mix
1 (8 ounce) carton whipped topping
36 vanilla wafers
3 bananas

In large bowl, combine condensed milk and water. Add pudding
mix and beat well. Chill 5 minutes and fold in whipped topping.
Spoon 1 cup pudding mixture into 3-quart glass serving bowl.

Top with wafers, bananas and pudding. Repeat layers twice and
end with pudding. Cover and keep chilled.

Bread Pudding With Whiskey Sauce

1 loaf French bread
1 quart milk
3 eggs
2 cups sugar
2 tablespoons vanilla
3 tablespoons butter, melted
1 cup raisins

Preheat oven to 350°. Melt butter in bottom of 3-quart baking dish and cool. Soak bread in milk and crush with hands. Mix thoroughly. Add eggs, sugar, vanilla and raisins and stir well. Pour mixture over melted butter and bake 55 to 60 minutes or until very firm.

Cool, cube pudding and pour into individual dessert dishes. When ready to serve, add Whiskey Sauce below.

Whiskey Sauce:

½ cup (1 stick) butter
1 cup sugar
1 egg, well beaten
Whiskey to taste

In double boiler, heat sugar and butter until very hot and completely dissolved. Add egg, beating quickly so egg doesn't curdle. Cool and add whiskey to taste.

Pecan Bread Pudding with Bourbon Sauce

3 eggs
1½ cups sugar
2 tablespoons brown sugar
½ teaspoon nutmeg
2¾ cups whipping cream
¼ cup (½ stick) butter, melted
½ cup pecans
½ cup raisins
4 cups Texas Toast, crust removed, cubed

Bourbon Sauce:

½ cup sugar
3 tablespoons brown sugar
1 tablespoon flour
1 egg
2 tablespoons (¼ stick) butter, melted
1¼ cups whipping cream
¼ cup bourbon

Preheat oven to 375°. In bowl, combine 3 eggs, both sugars, nutmeg, whipping cream, butter, pecans and raisins. Place bread in 6 x 10-inch loaf pan and pour egg-cream mixture over bread. Cover and bake for 20 minutes. Remove cover, cook another 30 minutes and cool.

For sauce, whisk sugars, flour, egg, butter and whipping cream in heavy pan. Cook over medium heat and stir constantly until mixture is thick. Add bourbon to sauce and mix well. Slice bread pudding and serve with 2 to 3 tablespoons bourbon sauce.

Old-Fashioned Rice Pudding

1 cup uncooked rice
1 quart milk
½ cup (1 stick) butter
5 eggs
¾ cup sugar
½ cup raisins
1 teaspoon vanilla
2 teaspoons cinnamon

Preheat oven to 350°. Combine rice and milk in saucepan. Bring to boil, cover and cook over low heat until rice is tender and absorbs most of milk.

Add eggs, sugar, raisins and vanilla to mixture and pour into sprayed 2-quart baking dish. Sprinkle cinnamon on top and bake for 25 minutes.

Sweet Potato Pudding

2 cups grated sweet potato
¾ cup packed brown sugar
2 small eggs, beaten
¼ teaspoon cloves
¼ teaspoon allspice
½ teaspoon cinnamon
½ cup milk
⅓ cup orange juice
⅓ cup (⅔ stick) butter, melted

Preheat oven to 350°. In bowl, combine all ingredients and mix well. Pour into sprayed baking dish and bake for 1 hour.

Buttermilk Ice Cream

1 quart buttermilk
1 pint whipping cream
1 teaspoon vanilla
¼ teaspoon salt
1 cup sugar

Combine ingredients and stir until sugar dissolves. Pour into ice trays and freeze. When cream is partially frozen, remove from freezer and beat. Return to trays and freezer.

Homemade Peach Ice Cream

1½ quarts mashed, ripe peaches
2 tablespoons vanilla extract
½ teaspoon salt
2 (14 ounce) cans sweetened, condensed milk
1 (12 ounce) can evaporated milk
½ cup sugar
½ gallon milk

In ice cream freezer container, combine all ingredients except milk and mix well. Add milk to mixture line in container.

Freeze according to freezer container directions.

Old-Time Peach Ice Cream

12 peaches, peeled, quartered
3 cups sugar, divided
Juice of ½ lemon
4 eggs
3 tablespoons flour
Pinch of salt
5 cups milk
1 pint whipping cream

Place peaches through blender and add to them 1 cup sugar and juice of ½ lemon. Chill.

Beat eggs slightly and add 2 cups sugar, flour and salt. Place mixture in double boiler. Scald milk and slowly add to egg mixture. Cook over medium heat in double boiler until thick, stirring frequently. Cool.

Place peaches, custard and whipping cream in ice cream freezer container and stir to blend ingredients. Freeze according to manufacturer's directions.

Samuel H. Rumph of Marshallville, Georgia is credited with creating the "Elberta Peach" in 1857 using a variety of tree seeds from his family orchard. One particular tree bore a truly beautiful freestone peach with excellent firmness, yellow flesh and crimson blush. Rumph named it Elberta after his wife. It is the most widely planted variety of peach ever introduced and is grown in all parts of the world.

Baked Caramel Corn

1 cup (2 sticks) butter
2 cups packed brown sugar
½ cup light or dark corn syrup
1 tablespoon salt
½ teaspoon baking soda
1 tablespoon vanilla
6 quarts popped corn
Peanuts, optional

Preheat oven to 250°. Melt butter in saucepan and stir in brown sugar, corn syrup and salt. Stir constantly and bring to boil. Boil but do not stir for 5 minutes. Remove from heat and stir in baking soda and vanilla. Pour mixture over popped corn and mix well.

Turn into 2 large shallow baking pans and bake for 1 hour. Stir every 15 minutes. Remove from oven and cool completely. Break apart and store in sealed containers.

The Jubilee Singers of Fisk University in Nashville introduced the beauty and tradition of the Negro spiritual. It became the basis for other genres of African-American music. Their successful tours to raise University funds during the 1870's set the stage for Nashville becoming known for its music.

Mother's Apple Crisp

6 cups Granny Smith apples, peeled, cored, sliced
¾ cup brown sugar
1 cup white sugar
1 cup flour
1 teaspoon cinnamon
¼ cup chopped pecans
½ cup (1 stick) butter, melted

Preheat oven to 325°. Place half apple slices in sprayed
9 x 13-inch glass baking dish.

In separate bowl, combine sugars, flour, cinnamon and pecans.
Mix well and pour half mixture over apples. Add remaining
apples and pour remaining mixture over top. Drizzle with melted
butter and bake for 1 hour, 30 minutes.

Tip: Serve with whipped topping or vanilla ice cream.

The most fertile land in Kentucky is in Barren County.
Bourbon County is dry and Christian County is wet.

Creamy Pralines

2¼ cups sugar
1 (3 ounce) can evaporated milk
½ cup white corn syrup
¼ teaspoon baking soda
¼ cup (½ stick) butter
1 teaspoon vanilla
2 cups pecans

In double boiler, combine sugar, evaporated milk, corn syrup and baking soda. Cook and stir constantly until balls form when dropped into cold water or until it reaches soft-ball stage on candy thermometer. This will take about 15 minutes.

Remove from heat and add butter, vanilla and pecans. Beat mixture until cool and stiff enough to keep its shape when dropped on wax paper.

Pralines

1 (16 ounce) box light brown sugar
¾ cup unsweetened canned milk
1½ cups pecan pieces or halves
1½ teaspoon instant coffee or freeze-dried coffee

Mix all ingredients thoroughly in medium saucepan, cook slowly over low heat and stir constantly until mixture reaches soft-ball stage. Remove from heat and set aside 5 minutes.

Beat with spoon until mixture is thick. Drop by teaspoonfuls onto greased foil. When cool and hard, peel foil from back and wrap each praline in plastic wrap.

Peanut Brittle

2 cups sugar
1 cup white corn syrup
½ cup water
2 cups raw peanuts
1 teaspoon salt
1 teaspoon vanilla
1 tablespoon baking soda

Combine sugar, corn syrup, water, peanuts and salt in heavy saucepan. Boil until candy thermometer reaches 293°. Cool until syrup spins a thread. Add vanilla and beat.

Sprinkle baking soda from spoon and quickly beat well. It will foam. Immediately pour onto well-buttered, marble slab, large cookie sheet or large aluminum serving tray. When cool, break apart and store.

Pecan pralines were an invention of Acadians among the parishes of Louisiana. So popular was the confection that it quickly spread wherever pecans were plentiful. Pralines quickly became a southern favorite.

Easy, No-Fail Divinity

2½ cups sugar
½ cup light corn syrup
½ cup water
⅛ teaspoon salt
2 egg whites, stiffly beaten
1 teaspoon vanilla
¾ cup chopped nuts

In saucepan, combine sugar, corn syrup, water and salt. Boil mixture about 4 minutes or until soft-ball stage.

In bowl, beat egg whites until fairly stiff and slowly pour half syrup into beaten whites (beat constantly). Continue cooking remaining syrup until it reaches crack-stage (270° on candy thermometer). While still beating on high, slowly pour in remaining syrup. Reduce mixer speed to low and continue beating another 5 minutes or until teaspoon of candy stands up. Quickly stir in vanilla and pecans. Drop on buttered baking sheet.

Tip: Soft-ball stage can be determined by dropping a drop of syrup in a cup of cold water (usually 234° on a candy thermometer). It will form a small ball.

When Georgia became the 13th colony, every man, woman and child was promised 64 quarts of molasses if they stayed one year. Molasses was the sweetener of choice until after World War I.

Old-Time Pull Taffy

2 cups sugar
½ cup light corn syrup
½ cup water
¼ teaspoon cream of tartar
½ teaspoon almond extract
Food coloring, optional

In heavy saucepan, combine sugar, corn syrup, water and cream of tartar. Place over heat and stir until sugar dissolves. Cook (DO NOT STIR) to 265° on candy thermometer.

Remove from heat and stir in almond extract and coloring. Pour mixture onto sprayed platter and cool. With greased hands, pull into ropes until chalky and porous. Break or cut into bite-size pieces with scissors.

COOKBOOKS PUBLISHED BY COOKBOOK RESOURCES, LLC

The Ultimate Cooking With 4 Ingredients
4 Ingredient Recipes And 30-Minute Meals
Easy Cooking With 5 Ingredients
The Best of Cooking With 3 Ingredients
Easy Gourmet-Style Cooking With 5 Ingredients
Gourmet Cooking With 5 Ingredients
Healthy Cooking With 4 Ingredients
Easy Dessert Cooking With 5 Ingredients
Easy Diabetic Cooking With 4 Ingredients
Easy Slow-Cooker Cooking
Quick Fixes With Cake Mixes
Casseroles To The Rescue
Kitchen Keepsakes/More Kitchen Keepsakes
Mother's Recipes
Recipe Keepsakes
Cookie Dough Secrets
Gifts For The Cookie Jar
Brownies In A Jar
101 Brownies
Cookie Jar Magic
Quilters' Cooking Companion
Classic Southern Cooking
Classic Tex-Mex and Texas Cooking
Classic Southwest Cooking
Classic Pennsylvania-Dutch Cooking
The Great Canadian Cookbook
The Best of Lone Star Legacy Cookbook
Lone Star Legacy
Lone Star Legacy II
Cookbook 25 Years
Pass The Plate
Authorized Texas Ranger Cookbook
Texas Longhorn Cookbook
Trophy Hunters' Guide To Cooking
Mealtimes and Memories
Holiday Recipes
Homecoming
Little Taste of Texas
Little Taste of Texas II
Texas Peppers
Southwest Sizzler
Southwest Ole
Class Treats
Leaving Home

cookbook
resources LLC
Bringing Family And Friends To The Table

To Order: *Miss Sadie's Southern Cooking*

Please send_____ hardcover copies @ $19.95 (U.S.) each $ _____
                    Texas residents add sales tax @ $1.60 each $ _____
                    Plus postage/handling @ $6.00 (1st copy) $ _____
                                $1.00 (each additional copy) $ _____
Check or Credit Card (Canada–credit card only)   Total $ _____

Charge to: ❏ MasterCard. or ❏ VISA

Account # _____

Expiration Date _____

Signature_____

| Mail or Call: |
| Cookbook Resources |
| 541 Doubletree Dr. |
| Highland Village, Texas 75077 |
| Toll Free (866) 229-2665 |
| (972) 317-6404 Fax |

Name _____

Address_____

City_____State_____Zip_____

Telephone (Day)_____(Evening)_____

- -

To Order: *Miss Sadie's Southern Cooking*

Please send_____ hardcover copies @ $19.95 (U.S.) each $ _____
                    Texas residents add sales tax @ $1.60 each $ _____
                    Plus postage/handling @ $6.00 (1st copy) $ _____
                                $1.00 (each additional copy) $ _____
Check or Credit Card (Canada–credit card only)   Total $ _____

Charge to: ❏ MasterCard. or ❏ VISA

Account # _____

Expiration Date _____

Signature_____

| Mail or Call: |
| Cookbook Resources |
| 541 Doubletree Dr. |
| Highland Village, Texas 75077 |
| Toll Free (866) 229-2665 |
| (972) 317-6404 Fax |

Name _____

Address_____

City_____State_____Zip_____

Telephone (Day)_____(Evening)_____